International Management and Production

Survival Techniques for Corporate America

For my parents,
George and Ida Plenert,
Who taught me the meaning of work.

International Management and Production
Survival Techniques for Corporate America

Gerhard Johannes Plenert, Ph.D

TAB Professional and Reference Books

Division of TAB BOOKS Inc.

Blue Ridge Summit, PA

TPR books are published by TAB Professional and Reference Books, a division of TAB BOOKS Inc. The TPR logo, consisting of the letters "TPR" within a large "T," is a registered trademark of TAB BOOKS Inc.

FIRST EDITION
FIRST PRINTING

A Petrocelli Book / A TPR Books
Copyright © 1990 by TAB BOOKS Inc.
Printed in the United States of America

Library of Congress Cataloging-in-Publication Data

Plenert, Gerhard Johannes.
    International management and production : survival techniques for
corporate America / by Gerhard Johannes Plenert.
        p.   cm.
    Includes index.
    ISBN 0-8306-7391-1 (H)
    1. Comparative management. 2. Industrial management.
3. Industrial management—United States. 4. Competition,
International. I. Title.
HD30.55.P54   1989
658'.049—dc20   89-33690
                                                 CIP

TAB BOOKS Inc. offers software for sale. For information and a catalog, please contact TAB Software Department, Blue Ridge Summit, PA 17294-0850.

Questions regarding the content of this book should be addressed to:

    Reader Inquiry Branch
    TAB BOOKS Inc.
    Blue Ridge Summit, PA 17294-0214

Vice President & Editorial Director: Larry Hager
Technical Editor: Roman H. Gorski
Series Design: Jaclyn B. Saunders
Production: Katherine Brown
Cover Design: Lori E. Schlosser

Contents

Acknowledgments

In order to give credit where credit is due, I would have to go back to 1978 when I was on the international industrial marketing team for NCR Corporation. I spent time traveling all over Asia, Europe, and Latin America. In 1980, I installed industrial systems for Clark Equipment Company in Mexico. Both of these organizations gave me the opportunity to make additional contacts and expand my information base.

In 1982, when I returned to the academic community, I expanded my international background at California State University, Sacramento, the University of Oregon, Brigham Young University, and the Colorado School of Mines. There are many names worthy of mention at every one of these institutions, such as Robert E. (Gene) Woolsey of CSM, but if I start listing them, I would be sure to leave someone out who is every bit as important as everyone else.

I also acknowledge the many authors whose reference material is cited at the end of the chapters. Their articles and books will be valuable to readers who wish to research a topic more thoroughly.

Lastly, but most importantly, I need to acknowledge my family, especially my wife, Renee Sangray, who will have to get used to living with me again, now that this book is completed.

Preface

This book was initially developed because I felt that a new philosophy for management styles has been emerging. This philosophy was triggered by the lack of United States competitiveness and productivity, and incorporates an international perspective.

The data-gathering process for this book involved several phases. Initially, I traveled throughout Europe, Canada, Asia, Latin America, and the United States to learn as much as possible about industrial management techniques. I found not just a few, but hundreds of available ideas. Nearly the entire chapter on developing countries, as well as the majority of the chapters on Japan and Europe, were written mainly from personal experiences. Unfortunately, many of the newly discovered ideas have not been proven with success stories and, therefore, were not appropriate for inclusion in this book.

The second phase of my research was a search of existing publications for successful examples of the various management techniques that I had selected. In many cases, what I found was more of a management culture or philosophy than a specific technique. The diversity of the countries in the chapter on Asia is a good example of different management cultures. Nevertheless, I described the culture because I felt that it was transferable to the United States.

Some management techniques were described, not because of their success but because of their failure. For example, the concept of noneconomic incentives is being fostered in the United States, but it has had disastrous results in Cuba.

The third phase of the research involved correspondence with many of the countries and companies of interest. From this I received additional information about management styles.

Preface

The book begins with the introduction of a new international management philosophy (chapters 1 through 3), a search around the world for new ideas (chapters 4 through 10), a summary of the ideas (chapter 11), the application of some of these ideas to developing countries and to the United States (chapters 10 and 12), and a positive look at the future for United States industry (chapter 13).

Introduction

Many books are published concerning management. They all explain the correct way to run an organization, from their individual points of view. Unfortunately, these books simply rehash ideas that go as far back as Henry Ford. It's time to realize that these old management philosophies are fine as long as all competitors are playing by the same set of rules. If all competitors believe in the same management philosophies, then it is simply the company that can do it best who will be on top.

Competition from Japan, Europe, Yugoslavia, South Korea, and many more countries is coming in forms that United States business hasn't experienced before. Additionally, management in high-inflation countries—such as Argentina and Israel—requires a change in ideas. In the United States, we have entered a new era of management—that of the "international manager." This is someone who not only knows the United States way of doing things, but who also knows the Japanese way of managing, the West German way of managing, or the style of any other country that this individual becomes involved with. This manager realized that no one style of management is "best" in every situation. Adaptive management is required. This manager needs to organize and motivate in a way that is related to his employees.

Along with this new "international manager" comes a new corporate philosophy. The tight, authoritarian control of managers and industries needs to be relaxed. Managers need to be allowed to manage with flexibility. Corporate measurement tools such as efficiency reporting, cost reporting, and ratio analysis are not appropriate to every management style. For example, a management style that supports a dramatic reduction of shop floor inventory will destroy employee efficiency standards and asset ratio analysis. The only corporate measures that will be appropriate for this futuristic manager are total revenues and total profits.

This book develops ideas that will make the United States become internationally competitive once again. It does this through the development of the "international manager" who uses ideas from all over the world. So, let's begin our search for new ideas. Let's search for excellence around the world.

1

Why "The World"?

The United States needs to become more competitive, both at home and overseas. To do this, the managers of United States industry need to do two things:

1. Remove existing biases about the "correct" way to run a business, and
2. Open the door to experimenting with new ideas, even if they initially seem a little far-fetched.

The first issue, that of removing existing biases in business, requires the elimination of ideas like the ones supported by Milton Freedman: that the primary goal of business is to make a profit and that all other goals are relatively unimportant with respect to this goal. This philosophy alienates workers and frustrates the ethics of the business community.

Another bias that needs to be removed involves the ideas of Naisbitt in *Megatrends* which stress that the United States is moving toward an information- or service-oriented society. This is to be achieved by sacrificing our industry and transferring the majority of it overseas. This presupposes several incorrect points, such as:

- That the United States manufacturer can no longer produce price-competitive products because of cheaper foreign labor, and
- That our economy can survive an almost complete dependency on manufactured goods from other countries.

The United States can and will maintain its industrial strength because the pain of dependency would be too great. Additionally, the United States is still the largest producer of technology in the world, and technology improves productivity and can reduce product price to the point where cheaper foreign labor no longer has a significant effect on product cost. This issue of a service- or information-oriented society is discussed in more detail in chapter 12.

Still another bias that needs to be removed is that the United States is the world's expert at everything. Not long ago, an experiment was performed which tested the ability of a grasshopper to jump. The process took ten steps. Each time the grasshopper jumped, one-tenth of its hind legs was cut off, and then it was encouraged to jump by having the experimenter yell, "Jump!". The length of each jump was accurately measured. Not too surprisingly, the grasshopper jumped a little less each time, until eventually he didn't jump at all.

The experimenters input the data on the grasshopper's size, weight, length, and many other relevant facts into a computer. They also input information about the length of the hind legs and the distance of each of the jumps. The computer contained an expert system based on artificial intelligence to help in the analysis. The analysis results were exciting and unique. The experimenters wanted their findings to be published in a major research journal so that everyone could receive the benefits of the analysis and make use of this new knowledge. The journal editors agreed, and soon the information was published.

Unfortunately, these results did not seem to have much appeal outside of the United States; developing countries did not seem to understand the significance of the work that had been done. So, the Americans attempted to "force" their new-found wisdom upon those that refused to accept the value of their research by telling them that if this new knowledge wasn't incorporated, funding to the countries would be cut off.

Thereupon, the research on grasshoppers was incorporated. Still, as the people of the poor, misguided, developing nations worked with this information, they chuckled as they read the results of the research project. The closing paragraph, in trying to explain the grasshopper's lack of ability to jump, read:

> It is the conclusion of this research that the shortening of the hind legs of the grasshopper has a direct effect on his hearing, and when the legs are completely removed, all ability to hear stops.

We may chuckle at the ridiculousness of this fictional grasshopper experiment, but we seldom realize that in the eyes of developing countries, there are many "grasshopper" stories in the business environment. One of the many hundreds of examples can be found in our obsession with labor efficiency. In the United States, we have developed numerous systems that monitor the performance and efficiency of employees. We often lose sight of the fact that in order to keep employees busy, they need tasks to perform. Another way of saying this is that we encourage our labor to be efficient at the cost of increased inventories.

The majority of the countries of the world are concerned with finding jobs for their people. Their biggest cost of production is inventory, not labor. To them, our labor-efficiency systems are grasshopper experiments.

A few years ago, United States and Japanese automotive manufacturers were competing head-to-head. The pricing of vehicles on both sides was fairly competitive. Then, suddenly, the Japanese were underpricing the United States auto manufacturers. Our automakers never knew what hit them, and dozens of excuses were created to explain this failure. The fact is, Japanese labor didn't become cheaper; the cost of Japanese cars to the American consumer remained about the same. It was the cost of the new United States car that had taken about a $1,500 jump in price. Why?

Looking at the numbers, we find that it's not direct manufacturing costs that have changed in the United States. The cost increase appears to be centered almost entirely in the increased cost of debt. For example, the high inventory levels of the United States automobile manufacturer is financed through loans. The interest rates of these loans took a sudden jump when the price of oil increased and inflation hit. This added to the cost of the American car.

Japan did not have the high inventory levels and, therefore, their costs to produce a car did not jump. Inflation has hit both the United States and Japan, but Japanese cars are priced competitively, and the United States is desperately trying to learn these cost-efficient Japanese production methods. (A more detailed explanation of the differences between Japanese and United States manufacturing systems is in chapters 2 and 6.)

This example illustrates that the changes that have taken place in the world economy have taken away the expertise of the United States to be competitive in the automobile industry. United States automakers have found it necessary to look overseas for new manufacturing management ideas. This demonstrates both points mentioned in the first paragraph of this chapter. First, it demonstrates that the American way of running a factory is *not* necessarily the best way to run a factory under current economic conditions.

Second, U.S. auto manufacturers found it necessary to open the door to new ideas, even if the ideas initially seemed a little far-fetched. Thus, the goal of this book is:

To help the management of United States industry become more competitive in manufacturing facilities both in the United States and overseas.

To achieve this goal, this book will investigate other countries throughout the world in an attempt to:

1. Generate new ideas for U.S. managers by looking at other countries' management styles and production methods.
2. Help the U.S. manager understand his foreign competitors better.
3. Internationalize the U.S. manager by offering a multitude of alternative explanations and solutions to the same problem.

Why should United States managers investigate the rest of the world for management styles? First, the "Shouldn'ts" of the American way of thinking restrict us from having an international perspective. This can be seen in the example of the American and Japanese auto manufacturers. (These "Shouldn'ts" are explained in detail in chapter 3.) Second, the United States needs to be on the alert for new and better ways of doing things. Third, the United States wants its domestic and foreign facilities to be the best-managed in the world. We can't accomplish this with a grasshopper-experiment mentality.

This book contains alternative management styles in three major areas of industry:

1. Production methods
   - Inventory management
   - Machine/equipment/facilities management
   - Labor efficiency management
2. Management/organization styles
   - Planning
   - Goals and objectives management
3. People management styles
   - Labor relations

Exciting new ideas have been learned in each of these areas, many of which are valuable in the United States and abroad.

My family got together for Thanksgiving dinner recently, and in addition to the traditional turkey, we were to have salmon. As my wife was about to cook the salmon, one of my sisters got excited, saying that in order to cook the fish properly, it had to be cut in half. With the fish cut in half, the two pieces could be cooked side by side. She insisted that this was the only proper way to cook the fish.

This bothered me, since I thought the fish would look much better on the dinner table if it were served as one piece, and so I asked my sister why it had to be cut in half. After some discussion, my sister finally admitted that the reason she cut the fish in half was because our mother had always done it that way. That explanation only succeeded in making me more curious, and so I called my mother to ask her why she cut the fish in half. Her response was the same. She did it because her mother had always done it that way.

Finally, my curiosity got the best of me and I called my grandmother to ask her why she cut the fish in half before she cooked it. Her explanation was simple and quite logical. She cut the fish in half because she didn't have a frying pan large enough to hold the entire fish.

I often wonder how much the "we've always done it that way" mentality prevails in our management systems. I hope this book will give you a new perspective on management styles and leave you with a larger frying pan.[1]

---

[1]Neither the grasshopper nor the fish story are true (fish stories seldom are). However, the message of each story is both true and important.

2

The Birth
of Many Methods

The American Production and Inventory Control Society (APICS) holds an annual international convention during which both new and old management methods are introduced to about 5,000 attendees. Participants come from all over the world to learn the best methods of management. The hosts of the convention have traditionally emphasized the "American" method of management, feeling that since our systems were developed by the most technologically advanced country in the world, they must be the best. Additionally, American systems use the most computer power, which is considered evidence that, because of its sophistication, it must be the "most correct."

Unfortunately, the Japanese are out-managing United States factories, and so consultants and managers have flooded Japan in order to learn their secrets. These "secrets" are regularly presented to this convention group. The convention attendees have been shocked to learn that the Japanese management system doesn't require a computer and is much simpler to use than its United States counterpart.

This left the representatives of the American style of management stunned. Had they been working hard in the wrong direction? Have business schools in the United States been teaching unnecessarily burdensome tools? The consultants and business schools immediately became defensive and developed elaborate schemes to try to prove that the Japanese style of management was really a subset of the good old American way and that the United States was just not using its style of management properly. They tried to explain how culture or economics wouldn't allow the Japanese methods to work for the United States. In their defensiveness, though, they missed the essential, underlying fact that Japan and the United States each developed management systems using a different set of assumptions. Each had a different set of problems and a different set of needs on which they built their management system. From these needs, each country developed an entirely different management style.

Why do different countries have different management systems? What are the assumptions that make a country's style different? Didn't the United States develop the "best" method for management? These are the questions that this chapter will answer, along with one other, the biggest question of all: Are the management systems used by different countries interchangeable?

American management systems go back to the industrial development era. Men like Fredrick Taylor developed systems that emphasized the efficiency of the individual employee. It was important to specialize the employee so that he could learn his job well, thereby allowing him to produce as much as possible.

In emphasizing employee productivity, two other elements of effective business management were ignored—materials and equipment. The Fredrick Taylor system did an excellent job of promoting labor efficiency, but what happened to the efficiency of the other two necessary elements?

The prime objective of industrial-era systems was to keep the employee busy, but in order to do so, it became necessary to stockpile inventory (better known as jobs) in front of his workstation so that he would always have plenty to do. It was considered nonproductive for an employee to wait for materials to arrive from another workstation. The inventory that was built-up required space for storage and needed larger buildings and more equipment for the movement of the materials.

It wasn't long before management realized that in order to make the employee as efficient as possible, there had to be some optimum quantity which the employee should produce. The search for this most efficient batch size resulted in the use of economic order quantity (EOQ) systems. EOQ batch sizes soon became the standard. This resulted in larger quantities of production (larger production batch sizes), which in turn resulted in larger piles of inventory sitting in front of each workstation, and then larger facilities in which to store all these materials.

During the 1950s we experienced the advent of the computer. It was then we realized that if product demand could be predicted (forecasting), then it was simply a matter of working backwards in time to compute how much labor, materials, and machine time would be required. It was no longer necessary to build in EOQ batch sizes, because now we could accurately predict *what* was needed and *when* it was needed. This new system was called material requirements planning (MRP).

However, even though the quantities of materials sitting in production had changed, the factory manager still retained his obsession with monitoring labor productivity. Efficiencies were established against which each employee could be measured. A good employee was one who consistently produced better than his standard rate of production. A good factory was one that was "balanced," which meant that it had no extra labor. The factory had exactly what it needed to produce the planned amount of finished goods.

Even though the MRP system greatly reduced inventory levels over its previous EOQ counterpart, it was still necessary to stockpile materials in front of each workstation. Each employee needed to meet his "standard" rate of production, but factory designers were not concerned with this additional demand for space. The United States had enormous expanses of land that weren't in use. Factories could easily be built a little larger to handle this need to keep the employee busy. This was considered a necessary cost of increased employee productivity.

This system, based on labor productivity with relatively little emphasis on materials and equipment, still exists as the standard for American industry. MRP, which came to life in the 1950s when computers became practical, has come under challenge in the 1980s. Inflation has caused high interest rates which are not expected to return to the lows they once were. So, how do these high rates affect the factory? Unfortunately, someone has to pay for the materials stored in front of each workstation, and someone has to pay for the excessively large factories. Since most of this cost is financed, the increased interest rates have caused these assets and inventories to cost more. This has affected the cost of the product enough so that many American products can no longer be produced competitively.

An investigation into the effect that management style has on production would not be complete without also looking at product quality. United States business schools have picked up on a concept from American businesses that teaches that an increased investment in quality may unnecessarily raise the cost of a product. This would make the product less competitive and less profitable. In many cases, the schools teach that it is cheaper to repair a few products later than to put more emphasis on quality up front. American businesses gamble on quality in hopes that the loss of customers through product problems will be cheaper than the expense of a higher quality product.

Having now reviewed the management style of the United States and having seen how this style has affected production, we will now look at the Japanese to see how their management style emerged. In the later 1940s and most of the 1950s, Japan was desperately trying to recover from World War II. It wasn't until the later 1950s and the 1960s that a management style began to emerge. In order to learn about managing businesses, Japan came to the United States, and here learned many basic principles. But Japan soon realized that it couldn't emphasize employee throughput at the expense of excessive materials or facilities.

The first problem they faced was land space. Japan's land mass is only about four percent of that of the United States. Therefore, facilities had to be built as small as possible and as close together as possible. Using this restriction as their guideline, they developed a management style that emphasized equipment and facilities rather than employees. By keeping factories small, they were limited in the amount of space they had available for storing inventory. In fact, they went to the extreme; they didn't want to store any inventory at all in the factory. They only wanted the shop floor to contain those materials that were currently being worked on. This, of course, meant that employees wouldn't always be busy since there would be occasions when one employee would be waiting on another.

Japanese management systems were then developed around this minimal-inventory philosophy. There were several results of this system in contrast to that of the United States. The Japanese had smaller factories, therefore lower overhead costs which needed to be applied to their products. They had less inventory, therefore lower inventory carrying costs. They were not affected by increased interest rates as dramatically as was the United States. However, their factories were not "balanced"; they contained excessive labor, but this was a cost that they were willing to bear. When inflation hit and interest rates shot up, Japan was better prepared to meet this challenge while the United States is still struggling with this cost today.

Since Japan had low levels of work-in-process inventory, it had no need for sophisticated computer systems to monitor this inventory. The total amount of time required for the manufacturer of a bicycle in Japan was less than one day, from start to finish, because it was continually being worked on. To produce the same bicycle in the United States takes about six weeks.[1] Additionally, many major industrial complexes in Japan are run entirely without the use of any computer system.

When considering Japan and the issue of quality, we can still recall the days of "Japanese junk" when Japanese products were not considered to be of much value. What gave rise to the new standard of quality? Practically all of the major markets for Japanese products lie outside of Japan. For the United States, all of the major markets for its products are within the country. Referring again to the business school concept for the cost of quality, we realize that repairs and customer loss are much more important to the Japanese who have to travel a long distance in order to fix a faulty product. Additionally, when national borders are crossed, maintaining a poor quality product becomes more difficult. As a result, Japan has become extremely quality conscious, whereas the United States maintains its emphasis on cost-justifying its level of quality.

One additional note should be made about goal-setting and how this affects the planning of the Japanese labor force. In Japan, there is a national goal of full employment. This goal is a government goal, a business goal, and a union goal. Because of this objective, it is easy to find employees that have been hired with-

---

[1]The difference in time results from the need for American products to be produced in batches. Then these batches wait in "queues" in front of a workstation until the employee is available to do the work. This queue time can be as much as 90 percent of the total lead time required in the manufacture of a product. The actual amount of time that the bicycle parts are worked on both in Japan and in the United States are comparable (see also footnote 16 in chapter 6).

The Japanese system has come to be known as JIT (just-in-time), so named because, in theory, inventory should arrive just-in-time for it to be worked on, and no sooner. The Americanized name for this system is "zero-inventory."

out any specific purpose or function. This would never occur in the United States where employee efficiency is critical. In fact, when considering United States goals, it is difficult to find many common goals among business, union, and the government.

Having demonstrated that Japan and the United States each came up with entirely different management systems during the same time periods (the last 20 to 30 years), it is interesting to further investigate this phenomena to see if it is also true for other countries. Did other countries also work with a different set of assumptions? If so, did they also come up with a different set of management systems?

The answer to both questions is, "Yes!" Each country does have a different set of assumptions, and each has come up with different management styles. This will be demonstrated with one final example, that of Israel.

Israel's growth occurred primarily after World War II, and its need for management systems occurred at approximately the same time as for Japan. Once again, we find Israel similarly limited in space, but it had two other influential factors that were even more instrumental in the development of its management systems. The first of these was brain power—Israel has the unique problem of having a population that is highly educated. So, to start businesses and develop management systems, Israelis didn't go to the United States or to Europe to learn; they simply analyzed the situation anew and developed their own techniques.

The second factor that influenced the development of Israeli management systems was its enormous inflation rate. Interest rates were staggering and money was very unstable. Due to this, the purchase of materials and the funding of inventory became a strategic part of the business management system.

What the Israelis developed was a system that emphasized low inventories, high throughput, and low operating costs. Their system was similar to the Japanese in that materials were a key element of management, but it differed in that the total economics of production was emphasized. Overall plant-wide profitability became the most important element of their system, unlike the balanced factory of the United States that over-emphasized labor efficiency.[2]

Let us review what has happened in each of the three countries. The major deciding factors for the management philosophies and the resulting management systems in each case are given in CHART 2.1. Using these assumptions, CHART 2.2 illustrates how each of these factors resulted in different areas of emphasis in the respective management styles.

From the almost simultaneous growth (the last 20 to 30 years) of management systems for all three countries, we now have three very unique and different techniques for managing a factory. There remains the important question

---

[2]One such Israeli system that has received much recent interest in the United States is OPT (optimized production technology) marketed by Scheduling Technology Corporation.

The Birth of Many Methods

United States
- Emphasis on labor efficiency
- Excessive land space
- Low interest rates

Japan
- Limited land space
- Long distances to markets
- Importation of energy and raw materials

Chart 2.1. Traditional Influencing Assumptions

Israel
- High inflation
- Excessive brain power
- Importation of energy and raw materials

that we began with: Are the management systems used by different countries interchangeable?

To answer this question, let's review what has happened to United States businesses in the late 1970s and early 1980s. As stated, the biggest recent event that affected product costs was inflation. High interest rates have caused the carrying cost of inventory to more than double, thereby driving up the cost of the products. However, this same carrying cost had an almost insignificant effect on the Japanese and Israeli management systems because low inventories were already a part of their management plans. When the costs of the inventories doubled, only an extremely small percentage increase occurred in the total product cost.

Since the United States now has higher interest rates, it is time to realize that some of its basic management assumptions have changed. No longer is labor the primary cost component affecting total plant-wide productivity. Inven-

Chart 2.2. Resulting Management Styles*

		U.S.	Japan	Israel
Goals	1)	Labor efficiency	Minimal materials	Economic efficiency
	2)	Balanced factory	High quality	Profitability
	3)	Profit	Full employment	
Organization Styles		Top-down	Bottom-up	Worker participation
Personnel Management		Domineering	Passive	Participative
Production Method		Push—labor-controlling	Pull—materials-controlling	Centrally managed—machine-controlling

The priorities on these goals come from the historic development of the management system. Assumptions have been made in the United States, for example, that labor efficiency improves profitability. This assumption is not true, but it has pushed itself into the forefront as a management philosophy.

---

*Each of the terms on this chart—including "push," "pull," and "centrally managed style of production control"—will be explained in more detail in the chapters on Japan and Israel.

10

tory carrying costs, especially that of work-in-process inventory, has taken on that role.

It is time for the United States to search for a system that will facilitate a new set of requirements. In the process of this search, it may well be that the existing Israeli or Japanese system, with some minor adaptations, will do the job. Perhaps there is another country that has developed a system that fits even more closely than either of these two. Let's move forward in our search for excellence around the world, a search for a better management system that will fit the United States and help it to become "Number 1" once again.

This chapter reminds me of a quotation from Albert Einstein that I like:

If you don't have imagination, all the intelligence in the world won't help.

Knowledge about specific management systems is not directly equal to success. It's only the first step. The way we apply this knowledge and use "imagination" is the final determinant of whether we return to being "Number 1."

3

The Shouldn'ts

A chief executive officer (CEO) from the United States was visiting one of his struggling facilities in a developing country. He spent the day going over the plant's books to determine why productivity was so low and why the plant was so inefficient. He decided that the factory needed more control in the areas of production flow and labor efficiency.

The plant manager was beside himself with frustration. How could he make his factory workers fill out more paperwork? Most of them could only read and write numbers. He saw the additional paperwork as another unnecessary slow-down of an already inefficient labor force, and he told the CEO how he felt.

The CEO saw the resistance shown by the plant manager as a sign of uncooperativeness. He told the manager that unless he started doing things the "company's way," he would soon be looking for another job.

This ate at the plant manager. He knew that he had to install the CEO's new controls, but he also knew that the information gained would be worthless. He decided to walk off his frustrations. After two hours of walking, he had only succeeded in becoming more irritated. He walked around the side of one of the buildings into a small passageway between two buildings and found himself face-to-face with the CEO.

The passageway was only big enough for one person. Someone had to back up. The CEO barked, "Get out of my way! I don't make way for fools!"

The plant manager, now madder than ever, slowly backed out of the way and said, "It's OK. I do!"

From this story, and many more like it, a list of "Shouldn'ts" was put together for United States managers (and CEOs). This list reinforces the two ideas introduced at the beginning of chapter 1, that U.S. managers need to remove existing biases and become receptive to new ideas in management styles. The Shouldn'ts are:

1. The U.S. *shouldn't* assume that all similar businesses or plants are run the same or that all people and markets can be negotiated with in the same way.
2. The U.S. *shouldn't* assume that it has the best method for everyone.
3. The U.S. *shouldn't* set itself up as the world's instructor; rather, it should play the role of student if it wants to be better.
4. The U.S. *shouldn't* assume that Japan just has one small trick up its sleeve and that if we learn it we will be as good as we once were or even better. As long as we are playing catch-up, caught-up is all the better we'll get. We'll never get ahead. Catch-up is just not good enough.
5. The U.S. *shouldn't* assume that Japan is the best or only model to learn from. There are many models, some of which are much better in specific situations.
6. The U.S. *shouldn't* live by the assumption that one method is good for everyone (MRP for the U.S. and JIT for Japan).[1]
7. The U.S. *shouldn't* assume that there is only one "best" model for running a factory, one best model for running a wholesale establishment, one best model for running a retail establishment, etc. There are many models, many of which have appropriate applications in various environments.
8. The U.S. *shouldn't* plan to lose its industry and be strictly a service society. Who wants to learn from a country that only teaches but can't be successful at what it teaches?
9. The U.S. *shouldn't* live by the assumption that by managing only one of the three strategic resources—(1) materials, (2) labor, or (3) machinery, equipment, or facilities—it will manage all.

Chapter 1 highlighted that the goal of this book was to help the management of U.S. industry become more competitive in manufacturing facilities both at home and abroad. To do this, the above list of Shouldn'ts must be incorporated into the manager's way of thinking to create a receptiveness to new, innovative ideas.

The solution to any problem first requires recognizing that the problem exists. That is the purpose of the Shouldn'ts. The sooner we recognize them, the sooner we can get to work doing something about them.

Let's take a closer look at the Shouldn'ts.

From Shouldn't Number 1 we learn that working environments vary dramatically from country to country. Hayes and Abarnathy are two Harvard University professors that recently raised some commotion by claiming that

---

[1]Chapter 2 explains MRP and JIT.

business schools are leading their students astray. They claim that schools are teaching management principles that are invalid and inappropriate, and that these principles are causing businesses to fail. This statement needs to be taken one step further. We need to realize that there is more than just the old and the new school of management. There are schools of management all over the world, each containing correct management principles to handle the appropriate management situation.

Shouldn't Number 2 tells us that there is more than one right answer, depending on who asked the question, where it was asked, and how it was asked. We only need to look at the multitude of systems implementing "correct American management principles" that are in serious trouble to realize that maybe we're not using the best management style in those cases.

Shouldn't Number 3 emphasizes Western arrogance. It's the attitude that we're the best so no one else has anything worth looking at. To understand the fallacy of this doctrine, all we need to do is list some of the countries that have become the best students of the world. Over the last 20 years the best students have been Japan, West Germany, and South Korea.

For Shouldn'ts Number 4 and Number 5 we need to realize that no one ever became great by imitation. If Japan has something we can use, let's not just learn from it, let's go one better and improve on it. Then we've achieved something worth looking up to. While we're looking so intensively at Japan, let's not forget Shouldn't Number 6 which tells us to look at other countries and other methods as well. There are several countries that are already looking beyond the goal of beating the Japanese out of some of their markets.

Shouldn't Number 7 emphasizes that in the investigation of numerous management methods, we should *not* look for the one best way of doing things. It simply doesn't exist. We need to recognize that there are many ways of doing things. Some are appropriate in some situations, and some are not. Our bag of management tricks should contain alternatives.

With Shouldn't Number 8, we can look at the current literature—for example, Naisbitt's book *Megatrends*—and see from this that current trends are heading us towards disaster. For example, the trend that the United States is shifting from an industrial society to a service or information society cannot succeed. The basic premise is that United States factories will move overseas and that megacomplexes will exist to service these many international installations. This trend means dependency for the United States. We didn't handle the dependency on foreign energy very well. Why should we turn all of our industry over to foreign nations and expect success?

Another fallacy that Shouldn't Number 8 addresses is that America's future service-oriented society is to play the role of teacher for the rest of the world's industries. Looking at this idea from the point of view of a developing country, it sounds like another grasshopper experiment. Already today, if a developing country were planning to build an automobile factory, would they go to the United States for the manufacturing technology? No way! So why should we think that in the future, when we have very few factories at all, other countries will select us as their instructors?

The last Shouldn't draws on the areas already discussed in detail in chapters 1 and 2, the idea of the three areas of management:

- Materials
- Equipment/machinery/facilities
- Labor

Each of the management systems listed in this book is oriented differently around these key areas.

The following chapters will address what systems have been successful worldwide. It would be impossible to touch upon every management technique that exists. Many had to be excluded simply because of a space constraint. However, this book is a collection of what was found of most interest and relevance to the United States.

This search begins with Western Europe and Canada. These countries contain systems that are familiar and comfortable to the United States. These countries provide us with variations to our existing systems. They are especially interesting in their socialistic people-management methods. Canada is interesting because it has used the United States as their teacher. They have improved significantly on many of our methods by learning from our mistakes.

From here, the focus will shift to Latin America. This region offers many lessons about developing-country management. Their culture differences allow for many interesting new developments.

The next two chapters are spent entirely on one country each, Japan and Israel. Each has production management techniques worthy of closer investigation. The rest of the world has already realized what most of the United States is still resisting. Japan is no longer an imitator; it is now an innovator.

Israel is an isolated and interesting case for several reasons. This country is a melting pot of many cultures and backgrounds, both East and West. Management systems developed there blend both styles. Secondly, as mentioned, the Israeli population has a high level of intelligence, and so many new ideas have been developed in Israel that other countries have not considered.

Asia is the present and future industrial power of the world, but to group Asians together as one class is highly unfair. Each country is quite different, and each offers much in new and upcoming management styles.

No analysis of world management styles would be complete without a discussion of the Eastern Bloc countries. From some of these countries we learn valuable lessons about what *not* to do. From others we learn interesting ideas about management-employee relations. The lessons are valuable.

Developing countries have a chapter of their own which discusses two examples of developing-country management and how it differs from Western methods. The message of this chapter is that many of the ideas listed in this book can be used to manage factories in such countries better.

The last three chapters summarize what was learned from the different countries and applies this to what is happening in the United States. Many of these tools can be implemented rapidly to help the United States regain its Number 1 industrial position.

4

Europe and Canada

Most Americans see Europe as the "Old Country." They see the development of new and innovative ideas as slowed to a snail's pace and feel that this is not the place to go in search of new ideas. West Germany is the only country with any strength in its currency, but they brought in most of their ideas from the United States after World War II. Canada is viewed as just a rubber stamp of U.S. methodologies.

In reviewing recent history, we find the attitudes stated in the previous paragraph are nearsighted. In reality, the United States' social patterns lag behind those of the United Kingdom by approximately 10 years. If this trend continues, we should pay closer attention to what is happening in the U.K. now and in Europe in general.

Other countries, like West Germany and France, have much to offer the United States in technology and "people-oriented" management styles. The mainland European countries give us a people-oriented perspective of Western management. The Scandinavian countries offer some interesting insight as to how socialism incorporates Western management philosophy.

Contrary to prevailing attitudes, Canada has much for us to learn. Since Canadians are given the opportunity to learn from our mistakes, Canada shows us how to implement many of our ideas correctly. This offers us the chance to improve what we have by studying their refinements.

UNITED KINGDOM

A closer look at the U.K. reveals that it suffers from serious labor strains. Labor bargaining involves negotiations with 10 to 15 labor unions in the factory.

Labor takes the communistic attitude that no legal and binding agreements exist. They can always break their negotiated agreements if they are not satisfied with the current situation. Under this structure, management is left without a carrot to entice the employee to work harder. In the strong adversarial relationship between management and labor, management is not free of blame. Management's tendency toward a strong, forceful, authoritarian treatment of the worker can be blamed for much of the resentment that the workers feel.

In the United Kingdom we find an interesting example of how a change in strategy helped to save a dying company and return it to its original leadership position. James R. Crompton & Bros. Ltd. was the leading source of teabag paper when, in 1972, C. H. Dexter, another teabag manufacturer, built a mill in Scotland. By 1980, Dexter had gained 60 percent of the market and Crompton's profits had dropped from £2.3 million to £10,000. Crompton decided to fight back in spite of the increasing cost of wood pulp.

The struggle to survive then went in an unexpected direction—Crompton decided to share his problems with his employees. Crompton got around the differentiation of employees with programs such as equality in profit-sharing plans. His employee involvement successfully reduced employee turnover and created a harmonious atmosphere. Crompton lead his sales force in an aggressive campaign in the marketplace.

Technological improvements also became a key ingredient in the return of this industry, including the computerization of many of the production functions. Crompton's commitment to his employees kept him from laying off any employees as a result of these changes. The changes just made the employees more valuable because of their additional training. The company even developed its own training programs.

Within the organization, employees were encouraged to become technical experts and were invited to study other areas of the plant by walking around and talking with other workers so that they could learn from each other. Crompton's managers at all levels were encouraged to spend time with employees at all levels.

Crompton won two victories in its battle against Dexter. The first was that it regained its lead in the U.K. market. The second was an increase in exports into market areas in the United States and Canada. It earned a return on profits of £1 million for 1981 and a continued increase from that amount ever since.

The key to Crompton's successful plan was their employee program with a promise of "full employment." This concept is also found in Asian and Latin American countries but contradicts the traditional United States philosophy of employee efficiency.

The United Kingdom has also been an interesting example of the struggles of workplace democracy. In 1977, the Bullock Report was heatedly debated, a move that planned to turn 50 percent of all corporate directorships over to the workers. This was hailed by unions as a major step towards workplace democracy, but was viewed by corporations as the first step toward financial ruin since it implied that investors would no longer be in control of their investments.

Some examples of workplace democracy already existed in the U.K. For example, the British Triumph Bonneville motorcycle factory in Meriden boasted that all managers and employees earned the same wages. Managers and supervisors were elected, and the jobs were rotated.

Another example of workplace democracy in the U.K. is the worker "takeovers" that have occurred in plants where corporations have planned shutdowns. The employees take over a plant and manage it themselves, allowing it to survive as a successful enterprise. If workplace democracy interests the reader, a more complete discussion of the topic can be found in the book by Zwerdling cited at the end of this chapter.

SPAIN

Spain also offers interesting insights into workplace democracy. In the Basque Region, a system of more than 65 cooperative firms exists called the Mondroagon System. This is a system of small cooperative firms which has grown to become major industrial strength in Spain. It includes agriculture, fishing, machine tools manufacturing, retail stores, a bank, and many products.

In the Mondroagon System, 10 to 15 percent of the profits goes to support social and community programs. Seventy percent is distributed to the workers of the cooperative as profits based on the number of hours worked. These funds, however, are not paid directly to the workers but are kept in a fund from which the workers receive approximately 13 percent interest. The funds can be drawn on or loans can be taken out. The remaining funds are held in reserve by the cooperative system for growth investment capital.

Management of the system is organized at a once-per-year election of the board of directors. These individuals then hire the rest of the managers. Managers are very conscious of their relationship with workers, since they have the potential of losing their positions each year. To the casual observer, though, this employee-owned cooperative has the same appearance as any other industrial organization.

Unfortunately, unlike Mondroagon, many of these worker-managed operations soon find themselves in financial difficulty. Some of the reasons cited include the lack of governmental support and the lack of interest of qualified management personnel to work for these types of enterprises.

BELGIUM

Belgium's version of the book *In Search of Excellence* is entitled *In Search of Belgian Excellence.*[1] The conclusion is that the United States and Japan are not the only countries blessed with excellence in industry. Belgium also has areas of excellence centered around several key items. Of interest are the following:

- Personnel motivation
- Specialization
- Simple structure
- Corporate pride

All of these can be considered areas where the United States might show improvement. The Belgian book lists specific companies that have been impressive by their performance in various categories.

Another interesting Belgian document discusses that country's strategy for industrial performance and progress. It is of interest to those companies dealing with countries of similar backgrounds to Belgium.[2] Some of the concepts this report highlights are:

- The political system and the company
- Production and marketing equilibrium
- Information systems
- Innovation in all areas
- The role of technology
- Decision-making and activities coordination
- Implications for Belgium

This 81-page report is in French.

SWITZERLAND

Switzerland has long been known as a country that sets the standard for manufacturing machine tools. It has also made a major international mark in various forms of process manufacturing. However, this expertise is so diversified

---

[1]*In Search of Belgian Excellence* can be sent for at the following address:

V. Brouwers, Conseiller scientifique
Federation Eds Enterprises De Belgique
4 Ravenstein, 100 Bruxelles

Or use the following telephone or telex numbers:

Tel. 02.511 58 80
Cable: FEVOBEL

[2]The document is also available from V. Brouwers and is entitled *Pour Une Meilleure Enterprise, Enterprises Performantes et Strategie de Progres.*

that I find it difficult to select a single company for investigation.[3] Let me refer the reader to a detailed source of additional information on industrial production in Switzerland.[4]

Switzerland exports about 70 percent of its production. Due to this high-export market, quality, delivery time performance, precision, reliability, profitability, and technical superiority are considered requirements for all they produce. For its small size (Switzerland's share of the export market is only two percent), it is amazing that Switzerland's engineering ranks near the top in a variety of tool products such as machine tools, textile machines, precision tools, printing machinery, and steam engines.

Swiss technology is amazing. For example, this landlocked country is the world's foremost supplier of marine diesel engines. Many nations have also taken note of Swiss research efforts in energy generation and distribution and in the electronics industry. However, the key to the Swiss success story is in their industrial research. In research money spent per capita, Switzerland ranks ahead of West Germany and the United States. Since the Swiss import most of their raw materials, their competitive edge must exist in the conversion of these materials into end products. They must be able to do this better than anyone else.

LESSONS OF EUROPE

Europe has many other management lessons for the United States to learn. For example, the concept of "cultural synergy," as fostered by Anton Stauffer of Switzerland and Robert T. Moran, suggests that synergistic effects can be gained when labor and management aim their goals in the same directions. To learn how to do this, they suggest looking at Europe rather than at Japan. Some examples of the lessons we can learn from Europe include:

---

[3]The average company size is 100 employees, and 97 percent of the companies have under 500 employees.

[4]The booklet *Switzerland Your Partner: Industrial Production* is available in English from:
Swiss Office for Trade Development
Avenue de l'Avant-Poste 4
P.O. Box 720
CH-1001 Lausanne
Switzerland
Other booklets that offer valuable information about Swiss industry include:
Swiss Technology—Top Technology
People Ideas Machines
Swiss Machine Tools at WESTEC '85
Switzerland Your Partner, Swiss Electronics Today
Switzerland Your Partner, Energy Generation and Distribution

Europe and Canada

1. The long-term planning timeframe of European corporations (about 12 years).
2. Decision-making which is done by a board of managers, rather than being centralized in one CEO.
3. The international orientation of European business.
4. A more social perspective, as demonstrated in France and Italy. Social and human relations are stressed.
5. Industrial democracy, as in Norway.
6. Job rotation and orientation programs which are common.

The cultural closeness between the United States and Europe allows for many of these programs to be copied and implemented directly from their European counterpart. The article by Robert T. Moran listed at the end of this chapter is a good starting point for anyone interested in learning more about these topics.

Wage Indexing

Lessons can be learned from Italy, Belgium, Denmark, Norway, and the Netherlands on the indexation of labor wages. Indexation resulted in stabilizing economic activity in these countries in the 1950s and 1960s. In the late 1970s and early 1980s, with the high inflation rates, adjustments had to be made to modify the indexing methods. From these countries we learn that indexes that are adjusted by external factors, like the price of oil, tend to raise wages unnecessarily. This in turn fuels inflation even more. Modifications have to be made to allow for external inflators.

Some countries, such as France, have almost completely dropped wage indexation methods because of their recent destructive effect on the economy. Many other countries have resorted to a wage-price freeze in order to kill automatic indexing. Perhaps our United States steel, auto, and rubber industries should take a closer look at what has happened to European indexing systems.

Pollution

The problem of pollution is related to the discussion in chapter 2 where I stated that different countries manage their industries with a different set of goals. For example, in the United States, where land is plentiful, hazardous waste is simply buried in some unused, isolated location. Unfortunately, growth has caused many of these unused areas to come into use, and now the hazardous waste is a serious contaminant.

In Europe, the use of landfills for the disposal of hazardous waste was never considered a reasonable alternative; land is precious and in demand. They proceeded to develop chemical treatment facilities which destroy hundreds of thousands of tons of hazardous waste annually. For example, 80 to 90 percent of the

United States wastes are dumped into landfills, whereas in Denmark virtually all chemical wastes are detoxified. Sweden, Denmark, and Finland, along with many other countries, have centralized high-tech treatment centers.

At first glance, it would appear that the United States has dropped the ball when it comes to hazardous waste treatment technology. It seems inconsistent that we would still be looking for dumping areas when improved processes already exist in Europe.

Nuclear waste technology is a special type of hazardous waste. It has also received a considerable amount of attention in Europe. In the United States, low uranium costs have made the reprocessing or permanent disposal of waste uneconomical. The spent fuel rods are stored in huge pools of water at the waste site.

For Europe, where no natural fuel supply exists, reprocessing is advantageous. The two reprocessing facilities in Europe (England and France) work together closely on technological developments. In Sweden, the disposal and management of nuclear fuels falls under the jurisdiction of the Swedish Nuclear Fuel and Waste Management Company which is developing technology for the long-term storage and disposal of these fuels.

Europe has other valuable lessons for the United States, which include not only how to dispose of hazardous wastes, but also how to fund it, what levels of government involvement are appropriate, and how sites are determined for the treatment plants.

Production Control

At Kumera Oy in Riihimaki, Finland, a periodic production control system has been implemented. This system helps to resolve a conflict between a long lead time for purchasing and a short lead time for delivering a product that is almost entirely custom-ordered. A finished goods inventory and fast customer service are not desirable in this environment.

Some features of the system include:

1. Reliable delivery lead time calculations.
2. The production plan reflects sales, finance, and engineering objectives.
3. Engineering changes are easier to control and don't have the drastic effect on scheduling that they used to.

Some key elements of this system include:

1. Product grouping for production parts which deals with production process similarities.
2. Production and resource planning are integrated with game-planning.
3. Production scheduling is done by production "groups."

4. Manufacturing efficiencies determine the sequencing of production "groups" for processing.

Some of the improvements demonstrated by the system include a four-fold improvement in inventory turnover and a total elimination of expeditors.

(*Expeditors* are factory-floor employees who "chase" jobs through the factory. When a particular job gets targeted for chasing due to its being excessively late or important, the expeditor's job is to follow the job from workstation to workstation, giving it the highest priority at each until it is completely through the manufacturing process. A production controller controls the production schedule. This individual follows all the jobs that are being worked on in the factory, making sure they are on schedule. He looks for ways to help those jobs that have fallen behind schedule.) Additionally, the number of production controllers was reduced from four to one.

Although the features of this system make it appear complex and sophisticated, the initial version of the system was totally manual. It was two years before it was computerized. Perhaps the complex and sophisticated United States production systems could also have been developed with a greater degree of simplicity.

Flexibility

Oy Wärtsilä Ab is another Finnish company that has found success through the constant pursuit of flexibility. During a time when many shipbuilders were struggling through a recession, this company found a niche in icebreakers and passenger liners. Today, Oy Wärtsilä Ab has the unique advantage of being a major supplier to countries in both the East and West, building ships for Britain and the Soviet Union from the same docks.

Wärtsilä's strength is in its flexibility. When everyone else was building supertankers, this company emphasized smaller specialized ships which are more difficult to build. When the market fell out of the supertankers, most of the other shipbuilders were not able to adapt to the change, but Wärtsilä was flexible.

Wärtsilä's flexibility can also be found in their management style. They were one of the first to incorporate the management circle techniques that are praised so highly in Japan. Their philosophy emphasizes project groups. Workers from various trades are taught problem-solving skills and how to handle work-site problems as a group. Managers, supervisors, and workers are put together into groups and become an interwoven unit working together on their daily routines.

Central production planning was also moved out to the work sites in order to improve flexibility. The step-by-step instruction process was simplified, reducing the paperwork necessary to build a ship by about 70 percent. Production and schedule problems are now resolved on-site, thus speeding up the resolution of problems and reducing the amount of forms necessary to report and resolve the problems.

Another step toward flexibility is the reinvestment of 10 percent of a group's income into new equipment and labor-saving devices. Cabin modularization is an example of such an innovation and has saved over one-third of the manufacturing time of a passenger liner.

Wärtsilä emphasizes that all senior managers should have some practical operating experience. Training sessions are provided to do this. In turn, lower levels of management are also allowed to give their input to upper management. This builds harmony and an attitude of entrepreneurship throughout the company by giving all employees at all levels the opportunity to interact with one another during informal sessions.

Interesting research on production and inventory control systems is being conducted in the Netherlands by the Ministerie van Economische Zaken. J.W.M. Bertrand has done work on the generalized development of production control systems. In his article, "Design of a Production Control System for a Diffusion Department," he doesn't merely give a solution to the problem, he develops a generalized approach for solving it.

At the University of Technology in Eindhoven, Netherlands, W. Monhemius is studying the development of production control systems. In his article, "Some Trends in the Development of Production and Inventory Control Systems," he compares three types of systems, those based on controlled situations, control systems, and mathematical models. He addresses the historical development of the different types of models and discusses how history has been instrumental in the design of today's systems.

Another area of production research developed in the Netherlands is the work done by Philips on flexible work systems in assembly. The assembly industry must be flexible in order to be competitive. Unfortunately, most assembly systems are very rigid with respect to changeovers. Philips has developed its own systematic, step-by-step methodology for this type of flexibility. Not only is the method workable, but it also allows for analyses of the economic and social aspects of the system.

IRELAND

Another country—seldom thought of as the local for modernized manufacturing—is Ireland. The reasons for placing facilities in this country are several, but key among them are the ideal working environment and entrance into the EEC (European Economic Community). International companies from the United States, Japan, Great Britain, and West Germany have set up plants that export 100 percent of their goods to other EEC members.

Ireland offers a blend of the old and the new. The most advanced machinery and work practices have been incorporated into this traditional, farm-like setting. For example, the American multinational Hyster has two plants that are running the JIT/KANBAN-type system. This should come as a great surprise to critics of this system that claim JIT/KANBAN can only work if all your vendors are sitting on your front doorstep. That is obviously impossible for a manufacturer in Ireland. For more information on Irish manufacturing, review the article by Spillane cited at the end of this chapter.

DIFFERENT NATIONAL GOALS

These examples of research in production and inventory control methods done in the Netherlands and in Ireland are typical of the research done all over Europe. As demonstrated in chapter 2, each of these countries has a different set of goals in mind. Often, the research done in these countries is tainted by United States management science experience. Fortunately, enough work is done that is totally unique and therefore offers valuable enhancements to our methods.

Norway

Norway has adopted a Work Environment Act aimed at reforming the work environment. A section of this act deals with work organization. It prescribes that jobs should provide workers with some degree of freedom and should allow workers the possibility of developing and maintaining their skills. Most have reacted to this law with skepticism, since this would be a difficult law to enforce. Still, positive changes have resulted from this legislation. For example, the unified effort of both the legislative and labor forces to improve the work environment is unique. Additionally, their efforts for constraints that are equitable for all industries shows concern for industrial competitiveness. For more information about this program, Bjørn Gustavsen's article listed at the end of this chapter is a good place to start.

If I were to ask, "Where was the world's first 32-bit super minicomputer introduced?" or "Where was the first multimode, multiuser operating system developed for a minicomputer?" very few individuals would think of Norway. However, Norsk Data has become one of Europe's leading computer companies. Pretax profits rose from 22.5 million (NOK—Norwegian Krönen) in 1980 to 233.0 million (NOK) in 1984 and earnings per share rose from 2.63 to 19.44 (NOK) during the same period.

Norsk Data's growth and standing is the result of many positive elements, including engineering and technological development. Of interest to us is the fact that if Norsk Data is compared with other comparable firms, the following results occur:

	NROE*	P*	OPM*
Norsk Data	23.9%	112%	15.9%
Wang Laboratories, Inc.	19.0%	98%	13.7%
Prime Computer, Inc.	20.5%	97%	11.8%
Tandem Computer, Inc.	13.0%	96%	10.0%
Data General, Corp.	18.0%	60%	9.8%
Digital Equipment, Corp.	12.5%	50%	8.0%

NROE—Net return on equity
P—Productivity
OPM—Operating profit margin

*Due to varying fiscal-year ends, all numbers are approximate for 1984 except for Norsk Data.

It seems clear from the data that United States computer firms are not as efficient in minimizing costs and increasing productivity as their Norwegian counterpart. This is occurring in spite of the fact that the majority of Norsk Data's customers are across national borders.

There are many lessons we can learn from this organization, such as:

1. An international perspective.
2. A management style that emphasizes delegation, which results in employee pride and motivation.
3. An informal working environment.
4. A working philosophy that says, ''It is more important to do the right things than to do things right.''
5. A majority of the employees are shareholders in the company.
6. A strong philosophy of decentralization to keep the company closer to the customer.

These ideas are also appropriate outside of the computer industry. By applying these techniques, other companies will have the opportunity to share in some of the success of this organization.

For those searching for a manufacturing software package, Norsk Data offers an MRP/Costing/Purchasing Control package tailored for European needs, with international considerations built-in. This package offers some features that any internationally oriented United States company should investigate.

Sweden

Sweden maintains a highly socialistic culture which, to some people, means high taxation and a large public sector. To others, this means high social benefits. Unionization is also extremely high when compared to other Western nations. Fortunately, the people and the culture of Sweden are extremely consistent, thus reducing the problems of class conflicts that exist in many other countries.

In Sweden, the management and the workers have a form of co-determination. Employers and employees share in the decision-making process and also in the responsibility for the decision made. Employee-management disputes are settled in a Labor Court.

The Swedish firm Saab-Scania is an example of a European company that has decided to concentrate its efforts rather than to play the role of a massive conglomerate. It has focused its efforts on the automobile, heavy truck, and aircraft industries. This strategy is credited with producing an average 22 percent operating profit growth over a six-year period.

In addition to consolidation, Saab-Scania places eight percent of its revenues back into product development, about twice what most United States automobile manufacturers use. When its heavy truck division was struck by recession, Saab-Scania cut back production, only building in order to fulfill specific orders. Most other truck manufacturers took to price-cutting and were hurt by the recession; instead, Saab-Scania continued to increase capital investment during this time period.

Another Swedish automobile manufacturer, Volvo, has made its mark with a unique program for hazard management. Volvo is highly involved with the government in establishing meaningful safety regulations for automobiles. This program has always been far ahead of its counterpart in the United States, even in the early years of car travel.

Volvo has a safety program that includes an accident investigation group and a crashworthiness and post-crash engineering group. Their improvements emphasize not only crash situations, but also pollution requirements. They include a sophisticated information feedback system that incorporates quality corrections and improvements into the product engineering functions. Their systematized approach for error feedback and correction is possibly the most elaborate in the world.

When looking at Swedish quality, one cannot bypass looking at Victor Hasselblad AB's camera industry. This company has long outperformed the rest of the world in the race for quality, including the next strongest competitor, the Japanese. This, along with the free publicity it has received by being used in the United States space program, has left it increasing its market share when other European camera manufacturers have been going downhill.

Hasselblad keeps its high level of quality by building a product that is consistent and not continuously reengineered. The company is not intrigued by stylishness. Additionally, 10 percent of the employees work full-time on quality control.

Like its Japanese competitor, Hasselblad works closely with its suppliers and continues a program of upgrading component quality. Unlike the Japanese,

Hasselblad sticks with a consistent, reliable product that it can make better than anyone else.

Sagging productivity is a problem that is affecting most Western nations. In the United States, the solution to sagging productivity is centered around increased automation or some form of profit-sharing program. In Sweden, we find a different form of incentive program. Their programs emphasize "helping" the employee to be happier in his work, thereby motivating him to work harder. This includes some of the following:

- Labor-saving equipment to make the job less strenuous.
- Worker teams (this originated in Sweden, not Japan).
- Job enrichment with cleaner factories, free leisure facilities, and comfortable, gardened rest areas.

Sweden has installed some of the most advanced materials-movement systems in the world. A good place to start researching these systems is Bruce Barger's article listed at the end of this chapter. For readers who are specifically interested in the production control methodologies of Sweden, refer to the publication by Jan Olhager and Birger Rapp or the publication by W. Bruggeman and R. Van Dierdonck at the end of this chapter.[5] Sweden's production control systems are based on materials requirements planning (MRP) as are most European systems. However, they include some interesting variations worth investigating further.

West Germany

West Germany is a blend of many different cultures thrown together as the result of two world wars and the following surge in industrial growth. This nation has grown to become the third largest economic system in the world, but is now facing reversal of this growth. The large labor force that was drawn into Germany during its growth and redevelopment has now become the reason for the high unemployment problem the nation faces. Germany became so accustomed to growth that it wasn't ready to manage a downturn in the economy.

When looking at the industrial sector, West Germany is difficult to analyze; it simply has too many successes in too many industries. Its broad range of engineering and scientific capabilities has long kept it at the forefront of indus-

---

[5]Both publications can be requested using the following address:
Sven Axsäter, Professor
Tekniska
Högskolan I Lulea
Lulea University of Technology
S-95187 Lulea, Sweden

try, and a stubborn persistence has allowed it to accomplish many things that so many others have long since given up on.

This German stubbornness has also influenced some interesting philosophies on labor management. For example, the NCR Corporation factory in Augsburg produces small computers and peripherals, and is primarily an assembly operation scheduled by NCR's own MRP software package. They use a system of flextime where the employees are allowed to come and go as they please. The only requirement is that they work a specified number of hours per week. The decision of when to work those hours is entirely left up to the individual employee.

Flextime would frustrate most production scheduling organizations; it is simply not rigid enough. However, the benefits are a happier, more satisfied employee who is dedicated to performing well on the job.

Another trend that is occurring in Germany is the shift to a more decentralized style of management. A less authoritarian approach is being implemented in many factories where lower-level management makes some of the key decisions. This is a strong break from the traditional authoritarian approach. An example can be found in W.C. Heraeus GmbH, a family-owned metals conglomerate that has been forced to decentralize the decision-making process in order to be more effective and to foster growth.

One of the benefits of decentralization is a new level of communication among the divisions. They are now more responsible for their own successes, and they search for and share ideas with one another. This sharing has required a gradual break from the traditional allegiance-oriented way of thinking that the previous authoritarian management style fostered, but it is successful and is of great benefit to the organization.

Heraeus also introduced the Japanese quality circle concept which encourages a think-tank approach where employees get together to share improvement-generating ideas. The original motivation for this program was to improve efficiency and the idea-generation process. An additional surprising result was that absenteeism dropped from six to four percent.

A system of co-determination, called *mitbestimmunig*, was first developed in West Germany in 1848 and was reestablished after World War II. It is now a part of the West German constitution. Under this concept, workers and shareholders share in the decision-making process of the corporation. A government-legislated formula specifies what the worker representation will be on the boards of each company (what percentage of the board will be workers). Shareholder and worker representatives are elected to their board posts and have equal voting power in the decision-making process.

As idealistic as the co-determination process sounds, it has been threatened recently by Germany's economic downswing. High inflation and high unemployment have caused worker unrest and dissatisfaction, alienating the workers and management. In many cases, management has started taking a firm stand against this concept, feeling that it is only workable when everyone benefits, but that when it comes time for hard decisions about employment and shutdowns, the decision negotiation process becomes bogged down because the worker representatives become personally involved and emotional, and decisions are no longer rational.

German technology is so abundant that no individual area stands out. However, sources exist that provide United States business with tools with which to learn more. Here are a few:

1. Price Waterhouse provides two excellent books for doing business in Germany, among other countries. These guides are intended to help educate United States businesses about the legalities and tax considerations, but they also provide interesting background about Germany. These books are *Meeting German Business* and *Doing Business in Germany*, and can be acquired through Price Waterhouse or through the German American Chamber of Commerce.

2. The high volume of German technology has caused the country to become a center for trade fairs and expositions where the nation can sell its wares. There are literally hundreds of international trade fairs in Germany each year. Two booklets will help you learn about these fairs: *International Trade Fairs Made in Germany* lists the dates and locations of German trade fairs and indexes them for easy use, and *AUMA Information Guide* provides the procedures necessary for involvement in German fairs and exhibitions.

3. The German American Chamber of Commerce helps United States businesses open a direct channel of communications with German businesses. They offer a service whereby you can call directly to this organization and get assistance in matching your problem with a German solution. Direct contacts in Germany will be supplied. This organization also works in market research and arranges trade show exhibitions. The organization provides weekly and monthly publications that contain business developments and background information. Offices exist in five cities: New York, Washington, Chicago, San Francisco, Los Angeles, and Houston. To help you get started, here is the New York address:

   German American Chamber of Commerce
   666 Fifth Avenue
   New York, NY 10019
   (212) 582-7788
   Telex No. 234 209

MRP

In the 1970s and early 1980s, the advent of high-speed computer processing capabilities saw the United States and Europe excited about material requirements planning (MRP). The United States emphasized a "regenerative" version. Regenerative MRP generates production schedules once or twice per week; net-change MRP regenerates production schedules continuously as changes occur in the factory.

It seems appropriate that Europe would select net-change. This software gives the impression of allowing tight control of production of the factory floor. Unfortunately, net-change systems require the accuracy of the production data to be somewhere around 95 percent. This level of accuracy works well in highly technical and clean environments, such as computer manufacturing, but it has turned out to be highly unrealistic in most other forms of manufacturing. The result is that many European facilities eliminated their net-change systems and opted for the regenerative version.

Regenerative MRP also requires a high level of data accuracy, about 85 to 90 percent. This level is attainable, but at an excessively high cost. This has caused many Europeans to look elsewhere for good but cheaper production control systems. Two countries with unique production systems that have caught the attention of the Europeans are Japan and Israel. Further explanations of what these countries do differently can be found in each of their respective chapters and in chapter 2.

Comparative studies of management style have determined that the United States management philosophy is significantly different from that in Europe. The following are concepts that the United States tends to agree with while Europe takes the opposing point of view:

- Conflict is valuable to an organization.
- More employee freedom of initiative does not require more control of the employees.
- Organizational structures where employees can have more than one boss are acceptable (matrix management).

Countries that tend to closely match the United States management styles are Sweden, the Netherlands, and Great Britain. Countries that have a management style that is most directly opposed to that of the United States include France, Belgium, and Italy.

Europe has much to offer the United States manager. It sets many of the trends that we will follow in the future. Its management maintains an international perspective and keeps international marketing in the forefront of all its planning. It is a showplace of human relationships and employee motivation programs that American management might fruitfully investigate. Employee involvement in management as high as the board of directors should also be considered by U.S. enterprises.

CANADA

Let's now move across the Atlantic to take a look at Canada. Canada has watched the United States and has seen our mistakes before it implemented its own management systems. In this way, Canada allows us the opportunity to look at improvements to many of our own tools.

Canada has high production costs and low productivity, as do many Western countries. This problem is magnified when we realize that Canada is highly dependent upon its export markets (primarily the United States and Japan) in order to stabilize its economy. High production costs make Canada less competitive. More and more of the burden of Canada's economic instability has been funded by increasing income taxes.

Canada's productivity runs about 25 percent behind that of the United States, and labor costs per unit of output run about 15 percent behind. In general, prices for Canadian goods tend to be higher than for similar goods manufactured in the United States.

Since the industrial picture of Canada looks so gloomy, why should U.S. firms be interested in learning from them? In today's international industry, many plants are installed in environments similar to that of Canada, where productivity is low and taxes are high. Still, many Canadian firms are very successful in this environment. By a closer examination of these firms, we can become more successful in similar environments, rather than using the environment as an excuse for failures.

Specialization

The Canadian companies that appear to be the most successful are those that specialize. These companies consistently seem to have lower costs and higher productivity than their larger competitors. The strategy seems to be one of cost reduction by mass production of a specialized product, and to increase exports in those cases where the Canadian market is saturated.

Companies that have oriented themselves toward specialization have experienced 20 to 30 percent cost reductions while at the same time increasing output as much as 300 percent. This takes advantage of economies-of-scale production and results in internationally competitive unit costs of production. These companies orient their employees, their management styles, and their training programs around their individual production "niches."

An interesting example of Canadian success is Ranger Helicopters. It found success in supplying helicopter services on an international basis, and is involved in energy and mineral exploration, fire fighting, and other similar areas. This company took a niche, learned what the needs of that niche were, and applied this knowledge to its advantage. The result is success when so many other Canadian companies are struggling.

Although specialization simplifies the production process, companies must retain the technological leading edge for their areas of expertise or else risk losing their markets to cheaper producers. Unfortunately, specialization forces Canadian consumers to go overseas for some of their needs, but ultimately, the increasing number of markets that are being taken over by specialized Canadian products offset the disadvantages.

In Canada we have an interesting example for those countries or companies that are currently in developmental stages geared around raw materials. A study of Canada's multinationals shows how vertical integration has allowed them to maximize the profits attainable from their raw materials industries. This is particularly interesting during a time of falling prices for raw metals.

In their research efforts, Rugman and McIlveen emphasize that a large United States influence exists in Canada, primarily due to its involvement in the Canadian economy.[6] Canada has successfully freed itself from some of this domination through the development of some 20 world-class, Canadian-owned multinationals. These companies started from a disadvantaged position, fighting off competition from the United States, Japan, and Europe.

In studying why these companies were so successful, several points of interest were brought out:

1. Eighteen of these companies are in resource-based industries and only two are competing in high-tech areas.
2. The companies started from an information-poor position and had to apply strategic management skills to position their products in various markets.
3. Trade barriers were difficult to crack in the highly competitive raw materials and natural resources market.
4. Multinational growth required these 20 multinationals to have 43 percent of their assets located in 13 foreign countries.
5. Firm and specific advantages in harvesting, processing, marketing, and distribution needed to be developed.
6. The internalization of those advantages was done through vertical integration to the intermediate product level. This allows a company to market its product at the most profitable vertical point and permits it to avoid the R&D costs of end product development.

Two of Canada's top 20 multinationals are high-tech companies: Northern Telecom (Nortel) and Moore Business Forms. Two more are distillers (Seagram and Hiram Walker), and two are brewers (Molson and John Labatt). For these, the competition is more intense than for the other companies, and marketing strategy is critical.

---

[6]Rugman, Alan M. and John McIlveen, "The Strategic Management of Canada's Multinationals: Who Needs High Tech?", *Business Quarterly*, Fall 1984, pp. 64-70.

The world's second largest aluminum firm, Alcan, is one of the four multinationals involved in mining, the others being Inco, which is the world's largest nickel producer, Noranda, and Cominco. These companies enjoy a proprietorship of natural resources and emphasize the vertical integration of their operations from the extraction phase through the preparation of formed metal products. This vertical integration includes the ownership of their own hydroelectric power sources. Competition in this industry is intense and substitute products are always a threat, but there are many lessons that can be learned from the way these Canadian raw materials industries successfully entered this highly competitive world market.

Small Businesses

In looking at Canada, it would be inappropriate to ignore the other end of the spectrum, that of small-business enterprises which make up 25 percent of the gross national product and employ 2.5 million people. Here is a country making giant steps toward multinational industrialization, yet the government hasn't forgotten the value of its small, growing industries.

The Canadian federal government has opened the Canadian Labour Market and Productivity Centre (CLMPC), which is attempting to share the responsibility for productivity improvements along with labor and management. In turn, all three sectors share the benefits. This program attempts to integrate the three major parts of an economy—labor, management, and government. In the United States, there are currently very few goals that these three organizations have in common.

EUREKA

European and Canadian industries are, of course, not trouble-free. They suffer from the same pangs of recession and low productivity that plague the United States. However, they are recognizing the problems and establishing strategies aimed at solving their problems. These strategies require a rethinking of their performance measures and establishing measures that emphasize an accelerated rate of growth. Measures such as customer delivery, manufacturing lead times, inventory levels, and product excellence have replaced the traditional measures of operating costs and employee efficiency.

In spite of all the references to technological advancements outlined in this chapter, European technology still lags behind the United States and Japan in many areas. To circumvent this, 19 European nations (the EEC, Sweden, Norway, Austria, Switzerland, Turkey, Iceland, and Finland) have joined to form a program called Eureka (European Research Coordination Agency). The hope is that by working together on mutual projects such as advanced fishing vessels, circuitry design, telecommunications, fiberoptics, crop genetics, and factory automation, the European community will be able to establish technological niches that will place it ahead of its American and Asian competitors.

Europeans are searching for a better way of doing things. They have used European, Asian, and United States technology whenever appropriate. If we learn no other lesson from Europe, we should at least learn to be receptive to what other countries can teach us.

REFERENCES

Anonymous. "Europe Breaks The COLA Vise," *Business Week*, February 7, 1983, p. 58.

Anonymous. "Revamping Organization To Handle International Growth," *International Management*, Oct. 1984, Vol. 39, #10, pp. 34-35.

Anonymous. "Norway—Program To Upgrade Industry Is Succeeding; U.S. Exports Boosted By More Affordable Dollar," *Business America*, Sept. 10, 1979, Vol. 2, #19, p. 22-23.

Applebaum, Steven H. and Donald Hinds. "The Role Of The Management Consultant In Small Business," *Business Quarterly*, Fall 1984, pp. 43-51.

Arbose, Jules R. "Hasselblad Comes Back Down To Earth," *International Management*, Vol. 37, #3, March 1982, pp. 42-43.

Bertrand, J.W.M. "Design Of A Production Control System For A Diffusion Department," *International Journal of Production Research*, Vol. 19, #1, 1981, pp. 1-16.

_____. "The Use Of Workload Information To Control Job Lateness In Controlled And Uncontrolled Release Production Systems." *Journal Of Operations Management*, #2, 1983, pp. 79-92.

Bruggeman, W. and R. Van Dierdonck. "Implementation Of Materials Management Systems," *Biblotheek voor Wetenschappelijk Bedrijfsbeheer*, Proceedings Of An International Workshop, May 26-28, 1982, pp. 2-47.

Daly, Donald J. "High Costs And Low Productivity Erode Profits," *Canadian Business Review*, Spring 1984, pp. 6-10.

De Young, H. Garrett. "Perspectives: Europeans Join Forces On Technology," *High Technology*, Oct. 1986, Vol. 6, #10, pp. 67-68.

Fieleke, Norman S. "Productivity And Labor Mobility In Japan, The United Kingdom, And The United States," *New England Economic Review*, November/December 1981, pp. 27-36.

Fishlock, David. "Nuclear Waste: How Europe Pulls The Dragon's Teeth," *High Technology*, March 1985, Vol. 5, #3, pp. 39.

Foundation Industrie-Universite. *Enterprises Performantes Et Strategie De Progres*, Universite De Louvain.

Gustavsen, Bjørn. "Improving The Work Environment: A Choice Of Strategy," *International Labour Review*, Vol. 119, #3, pp. 271-286.

Krause, Hans W. "Industrial Research Is Key To Swiss Success," *Textile Month*, April 1985, pp. 23-48.

Laurent, Andre. "Matrix Organizations And Latin Cultures: A Note On The Use Of Comparative-Research Data In Management Education," *International Studies Of Management And Organization*, Vol. 10, #4, pp. 101-114.

Lemaitre, Nadine. *In Search Of Belgian Excellence*, Maître de conféerences à l' U.L.B., Janvier 1984.

MacCharles, D.C. "Knowledge, Productivity And Industrial Policy," *Cost and Management*, January/February 1983, pp. 14-18.

Metzger, J.M. *Designing Flexible Work Systems In Assembly*, N.V. Phillips' Gloeilampenfabrieken, Eindhoven, The Netherlands, May 1982.

Monhemius, W. "Some Trends In The Development Of Production And Inventory Control Systems," *Production Management Systems*, 1981, pp. 53-56.

Moran, Robert T. "Theory Z: But Not Japan," *Advanced Management Journal*, Vol. 48, #4, Autumn 1983, pp. 27-33.

Novitsky, Michael P. "Lessons From Europe: What's Going On Across The Atlantic," *P & IM Review*, April 1985, pp. 40-69.

Olhager, Jan and Birger Rapp. *A Reference System For Manufacturing Planning And Control*, Linköping Institute Of Technology, Department of Economics, March 1985.

Piasecki, Bruce and Gary A. Davis. "A Grand Tour Of Europe's Hazardous-Waste Facilities," *Technology Review*, Vol. 87, #5, July 1984, pp. 20-29.

Raulo, Jarmo. "Data Processing—Experiences And Ideas In Kansallis-Osake-Pankki," *Kansallis-Osake-Pankki Economic Review*, 1983, #1, pp. 3-7.

Richman, Louis. "Saab-Scania Kicks Into High Gear," *Fortune*, November 26, 1984, pp. 105-112.

Rugman, Alan M. and John McIlveen. "The Strategic Management Of Canada's Multinationals: Who Needs High Tech?," *Business Quarterly*, Fall 1984, pp. 64-70.

Spillane, Maurice. "Manufacturing In Ireland," *P&IM Review*, October, 1986, Vol. 6, #10, pp. 35-36.

Svenson, Ola. "Managing The Risks Of The Automobile: A Study Of A Swedish Car Manufacturer," *Management Science*, Vol. 30, #4, April 1984, pp. 486-502.

Vander Doelen, Chris. "Cashing In On Copters: How The Pearce Brothers Took Flight," *Canadian Business*, May 1982, Vol. 55, #5, p. 34.

Van De Vliet, Anita. "How Crompton Took The Strain," *Management Today*, March 1984, pp. 58-65.

Warskett, George. "The Role Of Information Activities In Total Canadian Manufacturing: Separability And Substitutability," *Applied Economics*, October 1984, pp. 763-770.

Whybark, D. Clay. "Production Planning And Control At Kumera Oy," *Production And Inventory Management*, First Quarter 1984, Vol. 25, #1, pp. 71-82.

Zwerdling, Daniel. *Workplace Democracy: A Guide To Workplace Ownership, Participation, And Self-management Experiments In The United States And Europe*, New York, Harper Colophon Books, Harper & Row Publishers, 1980, pp. 144-158.

5

Latin America

In considering Latin American countries, our first tendency as United States citizens[1] is to say, "What can we learn from a developing country? They can't even make their own systems work?" This arrogance, though, is exactly what got us in trouble as a worldwide competitor. We didn't pay enough attention to what the Japanese were doing during their developmental stages, and now we're desperately trying to copy them.

During my Latin American travels, I had the opportunity to spend over 18 months working in a manufacturing plant in Mexico. Almost immediately it became apparent that the United States and British managers of the company treated each other differently than they treated their Mexican counterparts. It was also apparent that the Mexican middle managers worked with each other differently than they treated their employees. What caused this difference in behavior? In discussing this situation with some of the Mexican middle managers, I was told that the workers, because of their culturally different set of standards and low level of education, had to be dealt with at their own level.

Further investigation revealed that the average Mexican worker was hard to motivate. His goals were not to have a lot of money, but rather to enjoy his family. Work was something that kept him away from his family. Often, after he received a paycheck, he would disappear for a few days, reappearing only when it became financially necessary.

This is an example of a management system in Latin America that should be of interest to the United States. It allows for the management of large differ-

---

[1]It is important to distinguish between an "American" and a "United States" citizen. Latin Americans, Mexicans, and Canadians are also Americans, although the tendency in the United States is for the people to think of only themselves as "Americans."

ences in skill and education levels. Latin America has learned to manage this disparity, and it's a problem that the international manager often encounters. Still, the question arises, "Does this management style have applicability for the United States?"

The answer is, "Yes!" We often find situations in process manufacturing or in the extractive industries where this problem exists. The difference is not so much an economic difference as it is a social, cultural, and educational difference. Management may be far removed from its employees[2] and may not relate well with them. Additionally, the many cultural pockets that have developed in the United States have made it necessary to deal with a variety of goals and standards.

DEVELOPING A MANAGEMENT SYSTEM

In reviewing the countries of Latin America, I found Argentina, Brazil, and Mexico particularly interesting since they have shown the most progress toward development. Puerto Rico is also placed into this category because of its uniqueness, having all the benefits of the United States government (a wealthy economy) yet maintaining a Spanish culture. Most of the examples in this chapter will be taken from these countries and this territory, but this is not to say that the other countries of Latin America do not have valuable information.

Conditions

Let's first study some of the conditions under which the management systems were developed. One of the most crucial conditions is that of unemployment—all of these countries have large labor forces that have very limited skill levels. Therefore, a major goal of management is full employment.

The next goal is to become competitive in the world market. For many of the developing countries, this is not a consideration since they are struggling just to exist. However, for Argentina, Brazil, and Mexico, this is a realistic goal which often contradicts the goal of full employment in areas where—in order to be competitive—the acceptable level of quality requires automation. Puerto Rico does not have this problem since its major markets lie within the United States.

A consideration that affects management style are the debt levels of these countries. These debts cause restrictions on imports and encourage exports, causing management to be more product-specific in what it produces.

Another consideration is the stringent government influences on how funds can be allocated. Economic difficulties have forced the governments of these countries to develop legislation that forces their industries to make better use of

---

[2]On-site supervisors—such as shop floor supervisors—are included in the employee category.

their resources. High import taxes have created a thriftier management style that generates less waste, makes better buying decisions,[3] and maximizes the utility of those items that are purchased, especially in the high-tech areas.[4] The benefit of this government intervention allows the country as a whole to avoid compound transactions, where separate industries independently spend money on the same pieces of technology. It is preferable for only one company to import the technology and then to internally sell it.

Of interest in the Latin American environment is the government support of sunrise (new and aspiring) industries instead of subsidizing sunset (struggling and dying) industries. This encourages growth and development in a new technological frontier as opposed to encouraging obsolete industries and technologies to continue lingering on for the sake of their employees. Governmental financial resources are limited, and since the countries are trying to move forward technologically, the dying industries are left to die and the national effort is placed on those industries that show the most promise for the nation as a whole.

Puerto Rico

In the United States territory of Puerto Rico, we find the reverse of what is happening in many parts of the United States. Managers have seen the need for management styles to be culturally sensitive since there exists a mixture of two cultures, the Anglo-American and the Latin-European. The balance between these must be managed cautiously. These two systems have different values and therefore require different management techniques. By investigating the predominately Latin-European population and seeing how Anglo-American values have been forced upon it, we can learn what to expect within our own mixed-culture society.

For a manager to function effectively, he must have the proper understanding of his subordinates and must have established an appropriate relationship with them. In comparing two studies using the same surveys, one done by Haire[5] looking at management styles of the world at large and another by Lewis[6] looking specifically at Puerto Rico, we find that the Puerto Rican manager values his employees more highly in what he perceives to be their capabilities than do managers of other countries, including the United States. The Puerto Rican

---

[3]Quality products, maintainability, and adequate spare parts supplies are stressed in the purchasing decision as opposed to replaceability or technological obsolescence.

[4]"Roundup In Rio," *Datamation*, March 1983, pp. 189, 190, 195, 196, 198.

[5]*Managerial Thinking: An International Study*, Mason Haire, Edvin Ghiselli, and Lyman Porter, John Wiley and Sons, Inc., 1966.

[6]"The Effect of Culture on Management Style," David A. Lewis, Ph.D., *P&IM Review*, April 1985, pp. 34-38.

manager blends this strong belief in the individual with the need to share information with him, and also favors the nonparticipation of the employees in company matters. This attitude is similar to that found in developing countries.

Internal Controls

Another subject that was analyzed was the need for internal control. Here we find Puerto Rican attitudes are similar to those of the Latin-European population. Puerto Rican managers feel a need for a high degree of internal control, much higher than that felt by the United States managers at large.

Latin America has been considered the red-tape capital of the world, both in the business and government sectors. There seems to be an obsession with duplicate forms, rubber stamps, and clerk windows. However, rather than considering this as a reason to avoid looking at Latin America, let's consider what companies like IBM Brazil and Ultrafertil in Brazil have done in their debureaucratization programs. IBM, after reviewing its internal bureaucratic systems, successfully eliminated the use of 2.5 million documents per year. This reform has also been extended to Brasília, the government seat of Brazil, where procedures have been greatly simplified in the attempt to "liberate business." This was not a step toward automation, it was a step toward organization. Government and multinational business organizations in the United States could gain from this.[7]

ADAPTING TECHNOLOGY

Latin American management styles are able to adapt advanced technologies by modifying these to make them satisfy management's internal needs. Traditionally, the United States has been a major exporter of technologies and rarely an importer, but as we observe how the United States is now struggling to install Japanese production methods, we realize that perhaps the U.S. will also need to learn to be more adaptive.

Let's see what we can learn from Latin America about adapting. Latin Americans have learned that, for technology to be truly appropriate for their needs, they must not passively import it and try to apply it, but rather must become masters of the technology, An iterative process occurs when the technology is learned about and understood, adapted, installed one step at a time, and modified to best satisfy the needs of the users. The adapting and modifying can occur in several stages until the technology has finally been successfully implemented.

---

[7]"IBM Brazil Helps Tame a Bureaucratic Brontosaurus," *International Management*, November 1984, pp. 82, 84, 87.

An example exists in Brazil where Usiminas, a steel producer, had its first plant installed through the help of Japanese steelmakers. This included extensive training, including hands-on operating experience in Japan. When it became desirous to increase the plant's capacity, the firm first built up its technological mastery and only imported technical assistance when it became necessary to supplement its own engineering efforts. The result was that this plant successfully doubled its capacity. This was done primarily through internal innovative technological changes; no additional capital investment and no additional labor was required for the facility to double its productivity. This process took seven years, but the knowledge and experience gained by Brazilian industry became invaluable for future expansion and growth plans. This knowledge was then applied to build other similar facilities, not just in Brazil, but in other countries in Latin America as well.[8]

Similarly, a Mexican cement manufacturer transferred his construction technology to Mexico. Having thoroughly learned how the plant was designed and how it functions, he now successfully adapts and builds many additional cement factories at a reduced construction cost of 30 to 40 percent and at a reduction in start-up time of also 30 to 40 percent.

These examples and others like it have successfully broken many bottlenecks in plants, improved the use of by-products, extended the life of equipment, and have cost-effectively altered the product mix. Most of these changes were oriented toward achieving long-term national goals.[9]

The basic Latin American philosophy on the transfer of technology centers around a philosophy of "learning by doing." In their research efforts, Dahlman and Westphal came up with specific steps involved in the execution of a technology-adaptation project. These steps are considered necessary in order to make the project effective:

1. Preinvestment technical and economic feasibility studies.
2. Detailed studies leading to choices among alternatives.
3. Basic engineering of the core technology.
4. Detailed engineering to supply the technology.
5. Procurement of equipment and construction contracts.
6. Training of the plant's personnel at all levels.

---

[8]A detailed explanation of Usiminas and its experiences with the adaptation of foreign technology can be found in *Managing Technological Development*, World Bank Staff Working Paper Number 717, by Carl J. Dahlman, Bruce Ross-Larson, and Larry E. Westphal, pp. 2-10.

---

[9]A detailed explanation of these changes can be found in the booklet *Technological Effort in Industrial Development*, written by Carl Dahlman and Larry Westphal and published by the World Bank under their Reprint Series (Booklet Number 263). This booklet contains an extensive list of references for further investigation.

7. Construction and assembly of the plant or equipment.
8. Start-up of operation.
9. Troubleshooting, which brings back the emphasis of adaptation.[10]

In all stages, the doing is more important than the acquiring because of the learning process that occurs. Often, this will require sending nationals abroad to learn the technology thoroughly before adaptation is attempted. In this way, a thorough study of the technology's appropriateness is made prior to its purchase. For example, purchasing technology that is "current" or "best" is not often desirable because there may be some restrictions on the amount of information that the seller is willing to supply. It is often better to acquire technology that is older but completely available. By learning this technology thoroughly, the industry is ready to advance to newer and better methods on its own.

In Mexico, a chemical producer would purchase technology only in those cases where the supplier of the technology would supply knowledge about not just how to produce the chemical, but also about the details of the chemical reaction. In this way, Mexico was able to adapt the processes for its own needs and to maximize its own productivity. Another example is a Brazilian petrochemicals firm that found a French firm that was getting out of the same business and was therefore willing to sell its processes. Now this Brazilian firm builds many similar plants both at home and abroad.

As is far too often the case, the proper transfer of technology coincides with a slow growth in productivity. For example, Dupont installed three similar rayon plants, two in the United States and one in Argentina. Considerably greater rates of increases in productivity occurred in the United States plants over their Argentinian counterpart which, on the surface, would appear discouraging. However, rather than comparing these two situations, we should look at the fact that the Argentinian plant still had an average annual productivity increase of 3.6 percent, and this in spite of the need to learn about an entirely new technology. In fact, during the learning process that occurred during the first three years, labor productivity doubled.[11] CHART 5.1 lists some examples of impressive productivity improvements in an environment of technological transfer. From the few examples shown on this chart, it can be seen that although productivity improvements may be slow, they are consistent.

OTHER LESSONS TO LEARN

A mixture of other lessons can be learned from the Latin American manager. For example, Argentina, like Israel, has to fight an enormously high infla-

---

[10]*Technological Effort in Industrial Development*, Carl Dahlman and Larry Westphal, World Bank Reprint Series, Number 263, pp. 117-118.

[11]*Assessing the Performance of Infant Industries*, by Martin Bell, Bruce Ross-Larson, and Larry E. Westphal, World Bank Staff Working Papers Number 666, pp. 18-20.

Chart 5.1. Some Examples of Productivity Improvements. *

Country	Industry	Period	Category	% Increase
Brazil	Steel	1966-77	Labor	14.0%
			Capital	13.0%
	Machinery	1938-79	Labor	0.5%
Puerto Rico	Garments	1951-61	Labor	9.5%
Argentina	Electrical machinery	1960-68	Total	10.6%
	Metals	1960-68	Total	9.3%
	Chemicals	1960-68	Total	9.1%
	Machinery	1960-76	Labor	5.8%
	Oil refining	1960-68	Total	4.1%
	Textiles	1960-68	Total	3.0%
	Rayon	1941-67	Labor	2.3%

*Assessing the Performance of Infant Industries, by Martin Bell, Bruce Ross-Larson, and Larry E. Westphal, World Bank Staff Working Papers Number 666, p. 19.

tion rate. This makes the country extremely sensitive to imports, especially of raw materials. Brazil and Mexico have established technological information centers that provide technological assistance to small industrial users for a minimal fee. Other agencies subsidize the development of the users' technological capabilities.

Brazil has been hailed in Latin America as a success story of economic growth. In Brazil we find a country that deals with two distinct markets, a national market and a world market. Prices internally are significantly higher than they would be on an open and free world market. This is done by imposing import restrictions in an attempt to develop internal industries and to allow them to grow and improve at the expense of the local consumer. The government, because of its economic crisis, is not capable of financing growth in all industrial areas. Here are lessons that the United States government and industry should learn about the effects of import restrictions and price constraints, and how this significantly increases the free market prices of the products sold within the country.

Reflecting back on the factory in which I worked in Mexico, I remember it contained an education center where classes were continually being held for the benefit of the shop-floor employees. These classes included the basics in reading, writing, and math, and made the employee a better individual both in society and in the plant. This also offered the company an opportunity to cross-train the employee, thus making him valuable in many functions. These classroom experiences were instrumental in determining which employee had the most

Chart 5.2. Summary of Goals.

	Argentina	Brazil	Mexico	Puerto Rico
Full employment	•	•	•	•
Be competitive	•	•	•	
National debt	•	•	•	
Governmental influences	•	•	•	
Reduction of red tape		•		
Reduction of inflation	•			
Technological adaptation	•	•	•	
Support of sunrise industries	•	•	•	

potential for being promoted into positions of more responsibility. The emphasis on individual education is something that exists in many countries of the world, and may well be a key to many of the gains these countries have made on the United States.

As mentioned in chapter 3, we now see that the United States doesn't have the technology that's best for everyone. If it did, these countries wouldn't require so many years of adaptation and modification before the transfer of technology becomes effective. Rather than being the arrogant instructor, the United States should become the inquisitive student and learn what the Latins (and the Asians, as we shall focus on later) know about adaptation.

CHART 5.2 summarizes some of the goals that affected the development of the Latin American style of management. Much can be learned about people management styles and about the necessity of adaptability (fitting in with the culture and the technology) in management. Although the Latins might seem more relaxed in their business atmosphere, don't let that fool you. They are busy working to solve the problems *they* consider important.

REFERENCES

Anonymous. "IBM Brazil Helps Tame A Bureaucratic Brontosaurus," *International Management*, November 1984, pp. 82-87.

Bell, Martin, Bruce Ross-Larson, and Larry E. Westphal. *Assessing The Performance Of Infant Industries*, World Bank Staff Working Paper Number 666, pp. 18-20.

Burbridge, Marc. "Roundup In Rio," *Datamation*, March 1983, pp. 189-198.

Dahlman, Carl J., Bruce Ross-Larson, and Larry E. Westphal. *Managing Technological Development*, World Bank Staff Working Paper Number 717, pp. 2-10.

Dahlman, Carl J. and Larry Westphal. *Technological Effort In Industrial Development*, World Bank Reprint Series Booklet Number 263, pp. 117-118.

Fox, M. Louise. "Income Distribution In Post-1964 Brazil, New Results," *Journal Of Economic History*, Vol. 43, #1, March 1983, pp. 261-271.

Haire, Mason, Edvin Ghiselli, and Lyman Porter. *Managerial Thinking: An International Study*, John Wiley and Sons, Inc., 1966.

Hewitt, Garth. "Why Volkswagen Is Optimistic," *International Management*, October 1982, pp. 21-24.

Knox, A. David. "Resuming Growth In Latin America," *Finance and Development*, September 1985, Vol. 22. #3, pp. 15-18.

Lewis, David A. "The Effect of Culture on Management Style," *P&IM Review*, April 1985, pp. 34-38.

6

Japan

Does Japan really have lessons worth learning? Does it have some "secret" methods that the United States needs to learn for it to regain dominance in the world market? In recent years, American managers and consultants have swarmed to Japan to learn its "secrets." With each visit, some new idea is learned, and they think they've found the answer to their problems. They return to the United States excited and eager to implement their new piece of wisdom, but soon find that it doesn't make them as successful as their counterparts in Japan. So these managers and consultants blame the cultural differences or the economy and conclude that the new idea will never work in the United States.

The answer to the difference in management styles between the United States and Japan is not found in the culture, although it is true that their Shinto religion probably gives them a greater dedication and drive. The difference is not economic, or any of the other dozen excuses that have been suggested. The difference is that United States managers have not been effective learners.

A common theme at many recent United States conferences is that in the implementation of improvements, the hardest "rocks" (the individuals that cause the most resistance) wear ties. It is not the worker but rather the manager that resists change. They would rather give up and say that the other guy's idea was no good than to admit that perhaps someone else might be smarter. So, many managers never look at the complete picture. They never realize that there are actually many pieces that make up the Japanese success story, and that all these pieces are integrated. Managers can't learn the success of the Japanese by looking at only one piece, because no one piece makes the whole system work.

This chapter will describe 16 techniques out of an initial list of over 100 that are in use in Japan (see CHART 6.1). Many of these are interdependent and need to work together for them to be successful.

When this chapter refers to successful "Japanese" methods, it is referring to those management techniques that are used in flow-production environments. These methods have been successful in large discrete [see footnote 4 in chapter 7—*Ed.*] assembly and fabrication plants. The types of products that are targeted by these Japanese industries are:

Radios	Televisions
Tape recorders	Binoculars
Cameras	Telescopes
Watches	Clocks
Timers	Bicyles
Motorcycles	Automobiles
Trucks	Ships

Chapter 2 introduced the development of Japanese management styles and pointed out that Japan has two key considerations around which it developed its management systems. The first consideration was land space, which is limited and therefore valuable. Considering this factor, anticipated improvements may be found in many areas, such as reductions in plant sizes, inventory levels, production times, and costs.

The second consideration was the distance to markets. These distances

---

Facilities Planning Techniques
• Shared resources
• Smaller factories
• Technology specialization

Production Planning Techniques
• Production sequencing
• In-line quality control
• Just-in-time or KANBAN
• Split shifts
• Lifetime vendors

Chart 6.1. Techniques Selected for Analysis.

Management Style Techniques
• Management circles or bottom-up management
• Statistical management
• Long-run planning

Employee Relations Techniques
• Lifetime employment
• No nepotism
• Profit bonuses
• Morale programs
• Employee rotation

---

force a higher level of quality because of a desire to avoid recalls or maintenance problems which would drive up costs.

Keeping these considerations in mind, a description of each of the selected techniques follows. They are grouped into appropriate categories.

FACILITIES PLANNING TECHNIQUES

Shared Resources

Two adjacent manufacturing organizations share such things as water towers, warehouses, waste treatment facilities, garbage removal facilities, transportation, power generation, maintenance, service personnel, a medical staff, and fire prevention facilities. By this consolidation of resources, they have one facility rather than the original two or more in each of these shared areas. This offers a larger and better-run organization for each of these areas. The result is a reduction in costs.

In the United States, organizations prefer to maintain independence. For example, if a particular facility wants to shut down operations, it would not want to maintain the cost of its portion of the shared costs for the common facilities. Additionally, in the United States, factories are not typically located close to one another.

The concept of sharing resources therefore offers Japanese firms significant savings in spite of its simplicity.

Smaller Factories

The Japanese can produce the same amount of output in about one-third to one-half the facility space that Americans use.[1] This smaller plant size is related to smaller inventory levels due to a difference in the production planning methodology. (For more information on how the Japanese reduce their total in-house inventory, read the section on production planning.) These inventory reductions have a direct effect on the size of the total facility by reducing storage space requirements.

Japan concentrates the type of work done within a facility. In contrast, a factory in the United States with several thousand employees typically includes at least a dozen departments. Each of these departments has a specialized function. For example, in a transmission manufacturing facility, the first department may be forging, the second may be sand blasting, the third may be grinding, and so on down the line until the transmission is completed. In each department is located all the equipment and manpower required to perform that function; for example, the lathe department would contain all the lathes for the entire factory.

---

[1]K.A. Wantuck. "The ABC's of Japanese Productivity," *Production and Inventory Management Review*, Vol. 1, #9 (1981), p.22.

Japan

In Japan, this same factory would be organized differently. It would be organized into several small factory modules, each doing all the functions necessary to build a specific type of transmission. These smaller factories would be organized by product line, rather than by function. For example, one of the small Japanese factory modules would produce a low-powered three-speed transmission, and this would be the only product that module would produce. This concept has come to be known as the *focused factory*.[2]

To do this, the Japanese have placed restrictions on their product output, one of which is that they limit the number of variations that are allowed. In the United States, a large number of variations are allowed, and these variations are usually a factor in creating large inventories in the facility (inventory must be stocked to handle all possible variations).

Small, specialized, product line factories are a viable and important technique for United States industry to study carefully. Managers and consultants have already attempted to copy this idea. They have named these American clones "group technology manufacturing cells" or "U-lines" to make them sound American, but unless the other tools that are listed in this chapter on Japan are also considered, the results that will be achieved will only be a small piece of the pie.

Technology Specialization

As previously noted, Japanese facilities are smaller and the equipment within these facilities is specialized for the particular function that the facility is performing. The United States concept of buying overflexibility does not fit into the Japanese plan where functionality and practicality are more important.

The Japanese use about 8,000 robots in their factories. This amounts to about three-fourths of the world's total population of robots, making the Japanese appear more technology-oriented than the United States.[3] They use conveyance equipment extensively, and buy very cheap specialized technology. The Japanese do not have employees unnecessarily moving parts or doing heavy work that could be more efficiently done by equipment.

Americans purchase multipurpose robots that can be used in many different places and for many different functions. The Japanese buy strictly what they need in order to perform a particular function and no more. This makes Japanese machines smaller and much cheaper, and more machines can be packed into the same space. This allows the Japanese to install monitoring systems which allow fewer personnel to oversee the operation of more machines than in the comparable United States facility.[4]

---

[2]Robert W. Hall, *Driving the Productivity Machine*, Falls Church, Virginia: The American Production and Inventory Control Society, 1981, p. 11.

[3]M. Shimomura, "What Makes Japan Work," *Science Digest*, Vol. 89, #10, 1981, p. 67.

[4]R.H. Hayes, "Why Japanese Factories Work," *Harvard Business Review*, July-August 1981, p. 60.

Additionally, because of the specialized machines that are used, rapid tooling changes are possible. This is one of the areas where the Japanese gain their quick machine-preparation time advantage. High-technology machines are not resisted by Japanese unions, and workers are not concerned about being replaced by machines. Employees encourage the installation of new technology and are excited about getting the most out of new technology. Employees work towards the improvement of the company as a whole; they believe that they are part of the total company. This worker/company attitude is discussed in more detail in a later section under the heading of "Lifetime Employment."

The Japanese use other technologies, such as group technology and conveyance technology, in their facilities.[5] They tie total computer-controlled operations together so that some production lines are completely controlled by computers, demonstrating that their technological advances emphasize both efficiency and effectiveness.[6]

Summary of the Facilities Planning Concepts

All three facilities planning concepts used by the Japanese have validity in the United States. However, they are not easy to install. The shared resource concept of the Japanese is probably the easiest to install in situations where facilities are side-by-side in the same area. The smaller factory concept requires a major reorganization of the facility. The specialized technology concept goes along with the smaller factory concept in that within the smaller facility all the technology is specialized for the one prime function of that area.

All three of the facilities planning techniques would reduce costs. The shared resources and technology specialization concepts would significantly reduce the number of personnel required.

PRODUCTION PLANNING TECHNIQUES

In Japan, production planning is done using the "pull" concept. Materials are not requested for work until they are actually needed and thereby "pulled" into production. The Japanese emphasize "just-in-time" production. This means that the materials arrive at a workstation just-in-time for the next production step.[7]

The comparable American concept is "material requirements planning." Materials are planned and scheduled based on an economic-order quantity and the parts are moved through the production facility in batches of this quantity. Materials are moved from one workstation to another and wait at each worksta-

---

[5]Hall, *Driving the Productivity Machine*, p. 19.

[6]Ibid., p. 7.

[7]More information about the "push" and "pull" methods of manufacturing can be found in chapter 2 and in the section on OPT in chapter 7.

tion until it is ready to work on the materials. This is a prime reason why American production lead times are so long.[8] This also causes a build-up of inventory and is why American production facilities require more space.

American production facilities emphasize employee productivity; they look toward making each minute of the employee's time as productive as possible. The Japanese emphasize factory productivity; the throughput of the "team," sometimes referred to as the "circle" of employees, is emphasized and must be as productive as possible.

Also essential to production planning is the efficient utilization of space. To do this, the Japanese "pull" production technology. When an order comes in for a product, it is passed to the final workstation which normally is an assembly workstation. Assembly passes the request for materials down to the next workstation below it and so on down the chain of workstations until it reaches the raw materials department which supplies the materials to the first workstation. This workstation produces a product for the second workstation and so on. The key principle here is that nothing is produced until someone requests a finished product.[9]

In the United States method of production control, a plan is generated for a given amount of time (6 to 24 months) listing the materials that should be bought. This is material requirements planning.[10] Long production lead times cause the purchase of enormous amounts of raw materials. Changes in the market or the product design result in an enormous amount of obsolete inventory. When the Japanese make a production change, all they change are the materials on which they are currently working. With only one to two days for their total production lead time, they do not end up with obsolete inventory.

In breaking down the production planning concepts into five key areas described below, we find that each element has some promise for United States production facilities. Each element can be used individually as a production planning concept, but using all elements together in harmony is essential to achieve what the Japanese facilities now have.

Product Sequencing

Product sequencing is the production of a product in one continuous flow, much the same as an automotive assembly line. Machines are lined up in the

---

[8]Lead time is the amount of time it takes to produce a product if it is manufactured. It is also the amount of time it takes to purchase a product from the time the order is placed until the time the product is received. Total product lead time is the total of all the production lead times and all the purchasing lead times for all components until a finished product is produced.

[9]In theory, nothing happens until a request is received. In practice, several requests are continually flowing through the shop and work is continually being done throughout the entire facility.

[10]H.J. Bromberg, "Inventory Planning—Basic Approaches That Still Apply," *Proceedings of the 21st Annual International Conference of the American Production and Inventory Control Society* (1978), pp. 725-730.

sequence of the production steps that are to be performed. This type of flow is used in all stages of the production process and produces the entire product in one continuous flow.

Product sequencing minimizes the lead time of a product. When we equate lead time to inventory and realize that inventory means invested monies that are doing nothing to help the facility and are often collecting interest charges, we realize that product sequencing can mean enormous savings in production costs.

In-Line Quality Control

With in-line quality control, every person on a production line is responsible for the quality of the total product (also called total quality control, or TQC). This includes not only each worker's particular function, but all previous functions. This requires that every production person understand how a product should look and perform before it arrives at his workstation. Each employee is responsible for making sure that all products meet the standard for work performed from the previous workstations, and returns work to the previous workstation if it has not been satisfactorily completed.

This function also involves the preventive maintenance of machines. Japanese machines look newer and run better than United States machines even when they are older. A better-operating machine results in a better product.[11]

In the current United States concept, whenever a job is completed on a particular product, the product is brought to a quality inspection area where it is inspected. After inspection it is sent back into production. This requires two material transfers and two material holding areas, and this results in a loss of production time because of the inspection, movement, and waiting times. To circumvent some of this lost time, several production steps may occur before each inspection. This means that if a mistake in quality is made in the first of these several steps, then several steps of production would be done unnecessarily on a bad product.

The Japanese concept of in-line quality inspection stops the product at the point where the mistake occurs. By catching problems earlier in the process they do not waste valuable time on worthless products. They also do not need the specialized quality inspection function where materials have to be routed, inspected, and then returned to the production process.

In the United States concept, it is quality control's responsibility to solve quality problems. It is seldom the responsibility of the individual worker that produces a product. This causes animosity between production and quality control and makes it difficult to identify and solve quality problems.

The Japanese are outperforming the United States in product quality. Their

---

[11]R.H. Hayes, "Why Japanese Factories Work," *Harvard Business Review*, July-August 1981, p. 60.

scrap rates are typically less than one percent, whereas comparable scrap rates for the United States are around 10 percent of total production. Scrap rates signify a waste of production time, employee time, and materials, all of which add to the cost of products.

Just-In-Time (JIT)/KANBAN

Japan uses the "pull" method of production, often referred to as "just-in-time" production, and also known as KANBAN or SASI.[12] The Americanization of this concept is called "zero-inventory." All of these names describe a concept where materials arrive into production when needed. Materials do not arrive to support a desire to keep employees busy. The materials arrive only because a particular output product is needed; production only produces the required output, no more and no less. To produce more is to produce "waste."[13]

In the United States we use a "push" system of production called MRP (material requirements planning). This system defines the total requirements of a factory over a period of time. Orders for materials are made according to this plan, and the materials are then "pushed" into production. This system works well until marketing or engineering changes occur to the product, and then the system deteriorates. Black & Decker, a Class A MRP user, almost stopped using MRP because of this problem.[14]

The use of "just-in-time" (JIT) production methodology does not involve sophisticated computer technology. In fact, the majority of these systems installed in Japan do not use computer systems.[15] Instead, they involve a simple two-card system. One card flows through the production steps, and the other is used to request materials. Whenever a part is needed, the request card is sent to the previous workstation. That card then triggers the production card to move to the start of the production sequence which in turn triggers a different request card for materials. When these materials arrive, they start the production process. This flow of request cards and production cards occurs all the way through the production sequence.

With this methodology, it is common to find that products requested on a particular day are produced on that same day. In contrast, comparable products typically take 30 to 45 days to be produced in the United States.[16]

---

[12]Wantuck, "The ABC's of Japanese Productivity," p. 28.

[13]Ibid., p. 22.

[14]A "Class A" MRP user is considered to be a user of an MRP system that has all aspects of that system operating properly; R.W. Hall and T.V. Vollman, "Black & Decker: Pioneers With MRP," *Case Studies In Materials Requirements Planning*, 1978, p. 34.

[15]Wantuck, "The ABC's of Japanese Productivity," p. 24.

[16]The amount of time that a product like a bicycle is actually worked on is three to four hours. The rest of the time is move time (transfer time) or wait time (waiting in queue for your job to come up or waiting because the rest of the batch has to be processed at the same time).

One common way of interpreting the difference between the Japanese and American production systems is to talk about "safety systems." In the United States MRP concept, we have "safety stock," a buffer of inventory for protection against mistakes or problems in production. The cost incurred with this system can be enormous since it increases carrying costs and obsolete parts. As problems occur, users tend to increase the safety stock so as to prevent the same problem from repeating itself, making these inventory costs even higher.[17]

In contrast to safety stock, Japan has "safety time." In Japan, it is more important to have the employees available to produce the product than to have extra pieces of that product sitting around. The Japanese believe that extra time is cheaper than extra pieces of the product which tend to become obsolete and thereby worthless. This is especially important if the extra pieces are far along in the production process with a great deal of labor time already invested.

A thorough understanding of the JIT or KANBAN concepts alone could be the subject of a book. Fortunately, much has already been written on this subject. APICS (The American Production and Inventory Control Society) publishes a journal, a monthly magazine, and sponsors many conventions, all of which offer numerous explanations of the concepts. The APICS organization should be the first point of contact for anyone interested in more information on this subject.[18]

In summary, installing JIT or KANBAN in the United States will require some major changes for American plants.[19] KANBAN can be transferred to the United States if conceptual attitudes about how employees work and how production lines should flow are changed.

---

[16]Continued. In the JIT system, batch sizes are much smaller and there is no transfer time. Queue time is minimal. For United States MRP systems, these wait and move times are large because of the large batch sizes. The result is the long production lead time discussed in this paragraph.

This does not mean that the Japanese produce more per day. The number of bicycles manufactured may be exactly the same for both facilities. However, the total time from the time work is started until the time it is finished on a particular bicycle differs dramatically between the two countries.

[17]Bromberg, "Inventory Planning—Basic Approaches That Still Apply," pp. 725-730.

[18]The address of APICS is:

APICS
500 West Annandale Road
Falls Church, VA 22046-4274
Phone: (703) 237-8344
TWX: 710-832-0848
CABLE: APICS SOC HQ

[19]Robert W. Hall, "Stockless Production for the United States," *American Production and Inventory Control Society 25th Annual Conference Proceedings* (1982), pp. 314-318.

Split Shifts

The Japanese concept of split shifts is already getting attention in many American production facilities. It involves running two shifts per day rather than three. These two shifts have a two- to four-hour gap between them. When the employees are at work, they should be geared towards production and not the maintenance, modification, or inspection of machines. These functions are done during the time between the shifts.

With split shifts, fewer employees are required because of the elimination of one entire shift of employees. The duplication of setup or maintenance employees running around and getting in the way of each other is also reduced. This is due to their being able to have the gap between shifts to work on the machines without interfering with the production employees. Thus, fewer maintenance employees are able to accomplish more in the same amount of time. All of this comes from the Japanese emphasis on team productivity.

With this system, communication between shift managers is greatly improved. The managers from one shift can communicate with the managers of the other shift during the nonproductive period between shifts without having to worry about keeping operations moving. In addition, shift turnovers are smoother and more effective.

A major complaint in the United States is that the split-shift concept eliminates the possibility of a third shift. However, in recent tests in the United States, a three-shift environment was changed to two split shifts. A 25-percent labor cost reduction resulted along with a nine-percent productivity output reduction. The net benefit was a 16-percent overall cost savings. There was also an improvement in up-time (fewer breakdowns) of the machinery; up-time improved to almost 95 percent where previous up-time figures were about 20 percent less.

Lifetime Vendors

The Japanese hire a vendor for life. They do not bid contracts out every year searching for the best price. They believe that it is important to get the vendor involved in the final product, and this involvement begins with the design of the product. The vendor is thus partly responsible for ensuring that the product is as cheap, efficient, and easy to produce as possible. The vendor and the customer thereby become "partners in profit."[20]

The United States concept emphasizes that all engineering designs should be done by the facility that assembles the final product. This often causes poor designs to be forced on a vendor, resulting in higher costs.

In Japan, in return for the vendor's input into the design and production of

---

[20]Roy L. Harmon, "Update 1982: U.S. Adaptation of Japanese Techniques," *American Production and Inventory Control Society 25th Annual International Conference Proceedings* (Oct. 1982), p. 179.

the product, he is given assurance that he will continue to be the vendor for this particular product. A long-term contract (up to five years) is established. The vendor thereby becomes part of the company and is involved in the total project. The Japanese believe that this is better than getting low prices which may result in poor or unreliable quality.

The Japanese also prefer to have their vendors residing within close proximity to their factories, thus allowing closer contact. This keeps quality problems lower and offers the opportunity for more frequent product shipments, thereby keeping inventories lower.[21]

Vendor relations are important because the vendor supplies raw materials to the factory. (Raw materials are those materials to which the factory has not applied any labor; an engine is a raw material to an automotive assembly plant.) A problem at the supply end ripples all the way through the factory.

Overall, the Japanese concept of dealing with vendors seems to have eased many potential problems.

Summary of Production Planning Techniques

As we have seen, the Japanese have some interesting production planning systems. In-line quality control requires training, but the possibility of taking advantage of improved quality benefits is very high for the United States. Additionally, the low production-waste levels of the Japanese make this a desirable technique.

Just-in-time production is an entirely new and innovative methodology for American production scheduling. It requires some major rethinking of American methods for the installation of this type of system. Factories will require some drastic changes not only in the way they are laid out but also in management's method of planning. This technique has already had some success in the United States.

Split shifts are easy to implement; this has already been done in some United States factories. Since it has worked well, it should be considered for more factories.

The concept of lifetime vendors is difficult to implement because of the requirement that vendors live in close proximity to the factories with which they are associated. However, the Japanese have already demonstrated that this technique will work in the factories they have installed in the United States.

MANAGEMENT STYLE TECHNIQUES

Management Circles—Bottom-Up Management

In the Japanese environment, the social role is more important than it is in the American style of management. An example of this is the management cir-

---

[21]Harmon, "Update 1982: U.S. Adaptation of Japanese Techniques," p. 180.

cle which incorporates the employee as part of the production team. This is a new concept to Americans even though it is often claimed to be a copy of an old concept called "participative management." However, the Japanese system works and the American system does not. Let's find out why.

The Japanese use quality circles. "Quality circles" is a buzzword in the United States originating from W. Edward Deming's work on quality control.[22] However, quality circles are just a part of the total concept used by the Japanese. They also use what they call "management" or "productivity" circles (named "ringi" or "ringi siedo" in Japan).[23] These are groups of 10 to 12 employees who work together on a particular product line. These employees work side-by-side and solve problems to make their area more efficient. The term "quality circles," sometimes called "small group investment circles," comes from the fact that one of the subjects discussed is quality. The result is an impressive improvement in the quality of Japanese output, and therefore the name.[24]

Many other subjects are discussed in these circles, from an employee's personal life to the way the factory should be operationally organized, and decisions made by the management circles are implemented. This is different in the United States—we simply have a suggestion-box situation where management passively reviews the suggestions. They are not considered serious recommendations for implementation and are only occasionally implemented. In Japan, such suggestions are almost always implemented, unless it is impossible to do so, thereby giving the members of a circle an active part in what happens in the organization. In a majority of cases, employee suggestions have provided a savings in costs and have improved productivity and output.

Additionally, the concept involves bottom-up management. The management circle provides suggestions to the foreman and he implements them. The same procedure works in the office. A group of employees will work together in the collective decision-making process. Their recommendations are passed to their boss for signature and approval. Very rarely is a collective decision rejected by the boss. Typically, this decision is implemented immediately.

Responsibility is passed from the top to the lowest level. The layers of upper management are very thin and the layers near or at the bottom (operational management) have the most employees. Managers at the operational level are closer to and more involved with their workers. Since the lower levels are the decision-makers, there is not much need for upper-level managers.

This technique also involves a concept that has been labeled "small group activities" which is used in over two-thirds of Japanese factories. The small groups, or circles, are encouraged to use their creative talents and their high

---

[22]W.E. Deming, "On Some Statistical Aids Toward Economic Production," *Interfaces*, Vol. 5, #4, 1975, p.2.

[23]Hall, *Driving the Productivity Machine*, p. 9.

[24]Ibid., p. 16.

levels of education to come up with creative product improvements. Individuals are trained not just in the traditional quality control and production methods, but also in:

- Conference management
- Problem-solving skills
- Creativity skills
- Team building
- Leadership
- Sales and service

The hope is that individuals will become more participative, spontaneous, and creative.

Japanese management supports this methodology because they claim that the best suggestions come from the employees and not from the managers. By involving the employees in the decision-making process, they end up with better employees. Employees can think and innovate without preconceived prejudices. They come up with better methods and better suggestions for accomplishing objectives.

The quality circle concept has been installed in some United States factories and is working very successfully in a few of these installations. It is not as successful as in Japan because of our many misconceptions of how things should be done. Retraining employees and redeveloping management philosophy is a difficult and slow process, but it has worked in some cases and it can work in many more United States facilities.

Statistical Management

Dr. W. Edwards Deming wrote many articles, one of which is "On Some Statistical Aids Towards Economic Production."[25] His article discusses statistical management. It was initially published for prospective users in the United States but, unfortunately, the reception for his ideas was poor. The Japanese, who paid close attention to American thought, caught hold of these ideas quickly. They took advantage of some of his statistical concepts and brought him to Japan to assist in the implementation of his techniques.

Since that time, Japan has become very successful in the use of statistical management techniques. They found that, through the use of statistical management, quality control, error-spotting, and general facilities control are much easier. Fewer people are required to perform the same control functions. With charts and statistics on some key areas of the production flow, it is easy to monitor whether activity within the facility is inside an acceptable tolerance range.

---

[25]Deming, "On Some Statistical Aids Toward Economic Production," pp. 1-15.

In this system, there is less of an information-processing requirement since the information is selective and exceptional. When information is statistical and displayed graphically, it is easier to see whether it is in line.

Statistical management incorporates a drive toward improved quality and improved productivity. Within this drive exists a complete bag of tricks that have become industry buzzwords. Each of these are thought of as separate tools, but the intent is to use them together in some integrated form. Examples of buzzwords include:

- Process Management
- Pareto Charts
- Scatter Diagrams
- Histograms
- Trend Charts
- Control Charts
- Variables and Attributes Data
- Process Flow Charts
- Cause/Effect Diagrams
- Process Management Process/Model/Definition

Information about these techniques can be found in any good operations research text such as the ones included in the "References" section of this chapter.

Long-Range Planning

American stockholders want annual profits, so American managers gear their activities around these short-term profits. The history of American production systems within the last 20 years has demonstrated that these short-range objectives restrict productivity improvements. The capital expenditures required to introduce advanced technology systems and factorywide innovations are too large to fit into an annual budget that demands profits. It has therefore become politically sound to modify outdated equipment and to receive the appropriate annual profits, thereby maintaining the goodwill of the stockholders.

The Japanese, in contrast, look towards the long-range objectives and are geared for large improvements on a long-term basis. This concept requires that all processes be analyzed carefully before implementation. Once implemented, they are not readily changed. In contrast, the United States makes changes to its production sequence on as much as a daily basis. This is because products are introduced too quickly and are not engineered as completely and thoroughly.

In Japan, borrowed capital provides about 70 percent of the Japanese manufacturer's needs, and equity funds provide about 30 percent. The opposite is true in the United States. This leaves the quick profit-oriented stockholder with much less influence in the Japanese environment.[26]

It is difficult to say whether the benefits of debt financing over equity financing can be sold to American banks. However, if banks took on larger debt risks, businesses would be motivated toward long-term profits, thereby reducing the failure rate of some struggling United States businesses.

EMPLOYEE RELATIONS TECHNIQUES

Lifetime Employment

Less than one-third of the employees hired in Japan are hired on a lifetime basis; however, the effect that these employees have on the overall operation of a company is critical.[27] When one of these employees joins a company, they actually become part of it.[28] They have their entire future planned for them, including the methods of advancement and compensation. They receive their education, retirement, and levels of promotion all as part of the company plan. The speed at which they move along in their plans is based in some small degree on their own abilities.

Compensation is based on the number of years the employee is with the company. The employee is involved in a lifetime of training, cross-training, and learning about the company and its operations. He is not put into one job and left there, as is the tendency in the United States where, when a person is particularly good at a job, that employee remains at that job. The employee may be promoted vertically in the organization, but seldom is the employee integrated horizontally into the other functions of the company. In Japan, no lifetime employee stays at one position for any longer than a certain period of time, usually about two years. At that point, he is trained for a different position. In the United States, this is difficult because the cross-training would be expensive and the fear that the employee might not stay with the company is too great.

In lifetime employment there is no excessive and unnecessary competition among the employees. They work as a team rather than as individuals. They don't undercut one another. They are not worried about technological advancements which may cause them to be put out of a job. They know that they will always have a job, and so the technological advancements they promote are for

---

[26]G.W. Plossl, "Japanese Productivity: Myth vs. Reality," *Production and Inventory Management Review*, #9 (1981), p. 61.

[27]Hayes, "Why Japanese Factories Work," p. 63.

[28]Only males are given the opportunity for lifetime employment; it is not part of the accepted social role for females. Nonlifetime employees are primarily laborers who are nonpromotable and who usually have a limited education. They include seasonal workers from farms and women. Both groups are believed to have other social responsibilities and are therefore only "temporary."

their own betterment as well as that of the company.[29] Consequently, technological advances are highly encouraged.

Worker support and attitude seem to be more conducive to productivity in the Japanese environment. Also, the Japanese are not afraid to overhire. Quite often, it is possible to find employees that do not have a full function or a full day's work to do. This is because the employee's function may have been eliminated, or perhaps he was hired as an extra to begin with.

The Japanese consider their employees an asset, more so than their equipment. They value an employee at around $700,000 for a lifetime of service.[30] The company sees its employees as "one big family" with no need for "time sheets, time clocks, and labor unions."[31] In the United States, the employee is financially considered a repetitive cost.

No Nepotism

In spite of the strong cultural ties in Japan, the Japanese have a very strict philosophy against nepotism.[32] Relatives are not allowed to join in the management of a company. Relatives of bosses are normally not even allowed to work in the same company.[33] This is another reason why employees within the company remain strong in their desire to stay on a lifetime basis—they have no fear of being replaced or demoted by a relative move-in.

Profit Bonuses

The Japanese involve their employees totally in their companies. This includes profit bonuses for the performance of the team and for the company as a whole.

Although bonus systems are in use in the United States, they are not as widespread nor as elaborate as those of the Japanese. An entire work team may receive an expenses-paid vacation to Hawaii as a thank-you for good performance. American bonus systems emphasize management and not the employee, whereas in Japan the employee and manager get equal benefits for the success of the company.

---

[29]Typically, lifetime employment is only offered by the very large companies, and therefore the loss of a job due to company failure is not a major threat. However, should the company fail, lifetime employment would offer no assurance, assistance, or guarantees. The job would be lost. The employee would consider himself responsible for the company's failure and the resultant loss of the job. This problem has not yet been seriously dealt with.

[30]Hayes, "Why Japanese Factories Work," p. 64.

[31]M. Noda, "Business Management In Japan," *Technology Review*, Vol. 81, #7, 1979, p. 29.

[32]The concept of "no nepotism" refers primarily to organizations with more than 500 employees. Family ties are a very important part of small businesses (less than 50 employees).

[33]Noda, "Business Management In Japan," p. 30.

Morale Programs

Morale programs within Japanese firms are primarily designed to show interest in the employees. Exercise programs, special interest programs, family orientation seminars, company schools, company stores, and family outings sponsored by the company are some prime examples. All members of a family are involved with the company, and this emphasizes that employees have a lifetime relationship with it.

Moral codes are built into company philosophy, an example of which can be found at Matsushita with these guiding principles:

1. Make contributions to world harmony.
2. Display the true form of a human being.
3. Be fair about responsibilities to owners and employees.
4. Be successful in business by achieving goals.
5. Understand that profits are merely the reward for good service.[34]

Japanese unions support morale. "Everything depends on dialogue and trust. What is good for the company is good for the union," says Yoichi Takahashi, head of Hitachi's 70,000-strong labor union.[35]

The Japanese have pride in their work and are proud of their equipment; they take care of it as if they owned it personally. Additionally, they work in a no-crisis atmosphere, and this benefits them with fewer problems and better results.[36]

Employee Rotation

Employee rotation is part of a much larger program in the Japanese system which involves cross-training employees. Employees spend as much as 10 to 20 percent of their time in training programs. They are constantly being prepared for positions within the organization, and have no specialized career paths down which to move. Their career paths involve being transferred through all the various operations and functions of the company. The Japanese consider this an enormous benefit. As an example, operators of machines are able to make minor repairs and to do maintenance work.

At a minimum, 100 different labor classifications exist in the American factory. In contrast, a similar factory in Japan has no more than seven different labor classifications. This is primarily because, within these seven classifications, each person is able to do 20 to 30 of the functions that are uniquely defined in the American classifications. This is also possible because in the Japanese environment the unions are company-wide and not defined to any particular labor classification codes.

---

[34]Noda, "Business Management In Japan," p. 24.

[35]C. Bryron, "How Japan Does It," *Time*, March 30, 1981, p. 37.

[36]Hayes, "Why Japanese Factories Work," pp. 60-61.

Employee rotation leads to high morale, especially when the employees gain personal knowledge and not just company knowledge. For example, William S. Anderson, Chairman of NCR Corporation, states that:

> Millions of Japanese are fluent not only in English but even in third and fourth languages; how many Americans speak Japanese? Japan, with half the population of the United States, graduates almost twice as many engineers; that's a per capita ratio of 4 to 1. And in international testing programs, young Japanese run rings around American counterparts, not only in math and science subjects but in many other subjects as well.
>
> It's no exaggeration to say that Japan is today the most literate, best-educated nation in the world.[37]

This demonstrates a zeal for learning coupled with a sincere interest in the individual.

In Japanese companies, employee attendance in training and education programs is encouraged. Admiration is shown to those individuals that participate. The training facilities are superb, elaborate, and well-equipped. Catalogues are circulated that announce classes in all aspects of company activities. Courses are geared for all levels of salary and seniority and include courses in cooking, tennis, English, and calligraphy.

New employees start immediately in a training program during their first few months of employment. Their courses include company history, company policy, organization, business etiquette, and tours of company facilities.

Managers are taught all company functions. Problem-solving techniques are taught to everyone as well as performance-monitoring information. Each employee cannot only monitor his team, but the company as a whole, and thereby can look for ways to improve both.

The United States has much to learn about employee rotation and employee morale. Employees are hired to perform individual functions and if they do not perform well they are not considered as potential assets in other areas. The Japanese look to the employee as being valuable in many areas. They also realize that the employee is not capable of performing every function well, and therefore they seek to find those areas in which the employee is best-suited. The United States has not yet achieved this level of employee-company relationship. When it does, it will probably learn what the Japanese already know: The relationship between the company and the employee is critical to the stability of the employee and affects the productivity of the functions he performs.

Summary of Employee Relations Techniques

The Japanese management style is worker-concerned and does its planning based on the employee team rather than on the individual. It is dedicated to

---

[37]W.S. Anderson, "What We Are Learning From Japan," *Nation's Business*, March 1981, p. 40.

involving the whole work force in the operation.[38] Management does not spend as much time judging the performance of the individual worker since fellow workers on a team will take care of motivating each other. It allows stockholders to have less of an influence on the business since they are not as involved in the success of the business as are the employees. The United States needs to learn all it can about the strong Japanese employer-employee relationship.

SUMMARY OF JAPANESE TECHNIQUES

Having reviewed 16 Japanese techniques, let's now take a brief look at the applicability of these techniques to the United States. The three facilities planning concepts used by the Japanese are not always easy to use in the United States. The shared resource concept is probably the easiest to use when facilities are side-by-side. The smaller factory concept requires a major reorganization of the facility. The specialized technology concept should be installed in conjunction with the smaller factory concept.

All three of the facilities planning techniques would save materials and total facilities costs. The shared resources and technology specialization concepts would probably reduce the number of personnel required. All offer cost benefits for United States facilities and are therefore viable alternatives for implementation.

The Japanese have some interesting production planning systems. Product sequencing holds many benefits for the United States, especially with the potential of the U-line concept. Products can be sequenced and produced in U-lines with smaller factory modules.

In-line quality control will require training, but it has already demonstrated benefits in the United States. The low scrap levels of the Japanese should make this a highly desirable technique.

Just-in-time production will require some major rethinking of American methods in order to be installed. Factories will need some drastic changes, not only in the way they are laid out, but also in the management's evaluations of priorities. Its installation can be made using U-lines formed as group-technology manufacturing cells and controlled by KANBAN cards. In the worst case situation, factories may need to be rebuilt in order to install this technology. New factories can then be built from the ground up with the proper organizational flow.

Split shifts are easy to implement, and this has already been done in some United States factories. Since this works well, it should be considered for more factories.

The concept of lifetime vendors is difficult to implement because of the requirement for vendors to live in close proximity and be readily accessible to

---

[38]Hall, *Driving the Productivity Machine*, p. 7.

the user (factory). American manufacturers who serve as vendors will be hesitant to build new facilities unless they are given some assurance that they will be permanent vendors. American companies have not yet accepted the need to commit to a vendor for a long period of time.

In the management techniques section, we reviewed three types of management philosophies used in Japan. The first was the management circle which involves bottom-up (participative) management and the well-known quality circle concept. The second technique mentioned was statistical management. The third technique was long-range planning as opposed to short-range American objectives. Each of these techniques requires a limited amount of actual factory innovation. As a result, each offers the potential of enormous benefits for the United States. Each can be installed within current factories in some limited way. Some of the techniques, such as long-range planning, may require the approval of the stockholders. Other concepts, such as the quality circle, will require the acceptance of unions. There is some form of each of these techniques that can be implemented in every business in the United States, be it strictly in the office, strictly in the factory, or company-wide.

Lastly, we reviewed five employee relations techniques. We found that three of these techniques—no nepotism, profit bonuses, and morale pro-

Chart 6.2. Evaluation of 16 Recommended Techniques

	Desirable	Usable	Cost Reductions Materials	Labor
Facilities Planning Techniques				
1. Shared Resources	Yes	Yes	Yes	Yes
2. Smaller Factories	Yes	Yes	Yes	Yes
3. Technology Specialization	Yes	Yes	Yes	Yes
Production Planning Techniques				
4. Product Sequencing	Yes	Yes	Yes	?
5. In-Line Quality Control	Yes	Yes	Yes	Yes
6. Just-In-Time or KANBAN	Yes	Yes	Yes	Yes
7. Split Shifts	Yes	Yes	?	Yes
8. Lifetime Vendors	Yes	Yes	Yes	No
Management Style Techniques				
9. Management Circles or Bottom-Up Management	Yes	Yes	?	?
10. Statistical Management	Yes	Yes	Yes	Yes
11. Long-Range Planning	Yes	Yes	?	?
Employee Relations Techniques				
12. Lifetime Employment	Yes	Yes	No	?
13. No Nepotism	Yes	?	No	?
14. Profit Bonuses	Yes	Yes	No	?
15. Morale Programs	Yes	Yes	No	?
16. Employee Rotation	Yes	Yes	Yes	?

grams—are being used to some extent in the United States. The concept of lifetime employment shows some promise for being used in the United States, even though there is a difference in the relationship between employer and employee in Japan and the United States. The final employee relations technique involves employee rotation and cross-training. From this, the United States can receive major benefits. This concept goes hand-in-hand with many other techniques such as management circles, statistical management, in-line quality control, and lifetime employment, all of which would be more effective under this technique.

CHART 6.2 contains an evaluation of the 16 techniques that have been presented. It shows that each technique was found to be desirable for the United States; there are enough benefits in each to make the total Japanese management concept a serious consideration for United States industry. This chart also evaluates the usability of each technique in the United States and whether they are valuable for labor or materials cost reductions.

All of the areas mentioned as potential improvement areas have some benefit for the United States, although in some areas the cost may seem excessive. A key element to this information is the fact that without proper consideration of the personnel relationships, none of these systems will be effective. The Japanese believe that the key to successful management is in how employees are treated.

THE ROLE OF THE GOVERNMENT

We find it easy to criticize Japan for what we claim is governmental intervention and what has been labeled "Japan, Inc." However, the only crime that Japan can be accused of is that of having unity.

In the United States and in Japan, three major segments influence industry—business management, unions, and the government. Unfortunately, in the United States, each of these segments is battling for and striving for a different set of goals and objectives, whereas Japan searches for a common ground. In Japan, these organizations work hard to remove roadblocks and barriers in order to progress. They realize that they need each other in order to be effective on national, company, and individual levels.

The Japanese government has formed the Ministry of International Trade and Industry (MITI), a collection of business and governmental leaders that look for international market areas that show promise. They then target these areas and work as a national unit to make effective inroads. Examples of targeted areas are the computer industry, the automobile industry, the motorcycle industry, the steel industry, and the electronics industry.

If a MITI-type organization were to be established in the United States, businessmen would regard it as a bureaucratic farce and would then continue to do what they felt was best for their own interests. Getting United States business or unions to cooperate with this type of organization would be next to impossible. Each segment would feel a loss of freedom to develop and create on its own, and therefore there would be no unity and no common set of goals.

If MITI is doomed to failure in the United States, why do we regard Japan's unified efforts with irritation? The reason is that Japan has built strength in an area where we show weakness.

MITI has spearheaded Japan into national unity and superiority in many markets. Under MITI, Japan is now trying to standardize computer software so that all development can be centralized and that any software application can be used on any computer built in Japan. Attempts at projects like this in the United States are so tied up in red tape that they are quickly forgotten.

MITI has also spearheaded training programs that help personnel achieve success. It helps them strive for technological breakthroughs to make Japan a high-tech society.

From these descriptions, one would be led to think that Japanese industry is simply the puppet of Japanese government. However, what we find is that Japanese business is probably the most highly competitive in the world, surpassing even that of the United States. Once an area has been targeted, companies fight brutally with one another for the major share of it. Even within companies, the competition is intense between employees, each striving for recognition. The quality circles that we hear so much about are in reality teams of competitors that battle it out with other quality circles for championship prizes such as paid vacations. The seriousness and intensity of this competition makes our football games look like child's play.

The Japanese government sees itself as an aid and a guide to business, not as a controller of it. The simple conceptual difference, seeing itself as the "servant" of the business community, changes the outlook of the governmental employee drastically, and results in organizations that stress unity.

THE FUTURE OF JAPANESE TECHNOLOGY

Much of the current literature about Japan is oriented towards making the United States manager feel better. For example, the claim that the quality circle of Japan is just a variation of the concept of participative management is nonsense for one key reason: quality circles work and participative management does not. Regardless of the excuses for our failure, the point is made that we have a lot to learn from the way the Japanese are successfully implementing this procedure.

We can't avoid studying areas in which the Japanese have been successful by claiming that we once had a dream about the same idea. We must try to learn what we can in order to match their success, but even this is not enough. By playing catch-up, the best we can ever do is get caught-up. We must look to the future to see what Japan has planned next and whether there is anything we can learn from this information.

The first thing we need to do to stay in tune with our Japanese competitors is to look at their business publications. The Japanese are not secretive. The general attitude that the Japanese are just waiting for the United States to create new technology so that they can copy it is also nonsense. Technological development in the United States has become too slow to suit the Japanese, and they are branching out with their own developments. To find those Japanese publications that would benefit your organization, read through the article by Bruce F. Rubinger cited at the end of this chapter.

A student of Japan's future will find the Japanese involved in a tireless search for improvement. They never seem to be satisfied with a process, whether it is in production or research. It can be seen in their search for options prior to making any selection, and can also be seen in their search for new markets and for flexible products that will satisfy those markets.

Intertwined in this search for improvement is the need to simplify. The Japanese do not see high technology as an improvement unless the process is both better and easier. For example, if a new piece of equipment is installed in a Japanese factory, its maintenance procedures should not require any additional inventory of tools beyond what already exists. This can be contrasted with what happens in the United States where a new set of tools is ordered and a sophisticated database is established to manage the new tools.

Another example of simplicity intertwined with technological improvement can be seen in the way robots are installed. In Japan, robots are not allowed to do any more than the few specific functions for which they were planned. This is not just because the robots are simply designed, but also because the product and production process are simply designed. In Japan, the goal of manufacturing engineers is to have the least number of steps possible in the manufacturing process. For example, Sony's Walkman II personal stereo is assembled entirely on a single machine.

In looking to the future, one change that is destined to occur is an increase in advanced automation systems. Currently, the only computers that are found in the factory are the numerical control computers used with robots. Computers are not used for inventory management or production control. As the Japanese begin to implement computers in these areas, additional efficiencies and increased productivity should be anticipated. This is also expected to include plantwide Computer-integrated manufacturing (CIM) networks that incorporate computer-aided design/computer-aided manufacturing (CAD/CAM) capabilities. An example is at Hitachi, which has a common computer language for its robots, machine vision systems, and conveyor systems.

In the trend of using more robotics, Japan makes a distinctive effort to design all products so that they can be readily manufactured by machines. This often involves designing parts with ''handles'' so that robots can manipulate them easily. Assembly is accomplished with minimal robotic movement, and the robot is able to accomplish all functions from the same side of the product.

An element that keeps the Japanese ahead is their obsession with testing everything thoroughly. For example, Fanuc, a major manufacturer of robots, uses its robots to manufacture the robots. Robots in the plant outnumber people five to one. It is through the use of these robots that they have learned many of the improvements that are now a part of their products.

Another advance that will see more use in Japan is the multiarmed robot. One arm holds the piece and the other works on it. This eliminates the need for part-holders, part-feeders, and positioning jigs.

Still another robotic advance is the use of free-moving robots that can roll around floors, walk on stairs, or "spider-crawl" up walls. This requires both optics and the ability to visualize depth perception. Additionally, voice command control is anticipated.

Automation is considered one of the keys to Japanese industrial growth and is a necessity because assembly-line work is becoming less desirable. Automation goals of 100 percent white-body (before painting) assembly and 50 percent final assembly are common. This is quite a step up from the current eight percent of automated final assembly that most plants have.

A contrasting example of the need to automate can be found in the Japanese electronics industry. Epson dot-matrix computer printers and Sony's 3.5-inch floppy-disk drives are built largely on manual production lines. One explanation for this is that the assembly lines are staffed primarily by young women who have left high school, but who are not yet married. These women do not have a strong career path and receive a minimal wage for their labor.

Another reason for the slow move to automation in the electronics industry is the need for "clean" robots that do not generate dust from their moving parts. Such robots are twice as expensive as conventional robots, which discourages installation. However, the Japanese are developing product designs that have fewer parts and are easier to assemble. With these efficient designs, automated assembly will require fewer steps and will become more desirable.

Having achieved production superiority in many areas, Japanese producers now see their competitors trying to move in on their markets. The Japanese see themselves as being the future innovators, thereby also achieving design superiority. For example, they have taken the 50-cc engine from a little more than one horsepower to over three horsepower, and they expect to go to 4.5 horsepower in the near future. Although gasoline engine technology is already 100 years old, the Japanese feel that it has a long way to go before it reaches technical maturity. They expect their engineers to push harder towards a goal of better performance. They realize that being superior in production is only effective in the short run; the long run requires superiority in engineering as well.

In the field of composites, companies such as Fudow Chemicals have teams of researchers developing new and innovative ways to use reinforced plastics (RP). Out of this research has come a variety of production products that could formerly only be produced using metals. The plastics make them lightweight, corrosion resistant, and durable. Today, RPs have become one of Japan's most vibrant technologies.

Another Japanese technological strength is in the area of biotechnology. They do not have the edge on any major breakthroughs, but they do have the edge on production technology. Additionally, they maintain hard-working teams of engineers that are holding the watchful attention of this industry.

Diversity is also a goal of Japanese manufacturers. They see the need to spread into other market areas and to open up new areas that are not yet as competitive. For example, Japanese motorcycle manufacturers are eyeing the lawnmower, snowmobile, and outboard motor markets. They see themselves as major contenders, and possibly even as dominators of these areas in the near future.

Software is another area in which the Japanese feel the need to take a stronger foothold. One unique project fostered by the government's Information-Technology Promotion Agency (IPA) has established an organization called the Sigma team. This group's goal is the absolute, total compatibility of computer software across all Japanese hardware. This means that a software product developed for one Japanese computer would run on any other Japanese computer. The nationwide savings that this will generate in software development is astounding. A software package will not need to be redeveloped again and again for each type of hardware and for each vendor. This system will then be linked to over 10,000 software development workstations, allowing all development to be done through a common source. In turn, all developed software will then be available from a common source, and will be compatible, no matter which hardware is selected.

Other Japanese software vendors, such as NEC, are working diligently on software engineering. Their goal is the development of a variety of software systems that will automatically generate program code. They claim that these systems will boost programmer productivity between two to tenfold.

The numerically controlled (NC) machine industry is a high-tech industrial area where Japan has taken a strong leading edge, having captured two-thirds of the world's market. Their goal is a meantime between failure of 5,000 hours, which is exceptional for the industry. Additionally, machines are engineered so as to be easily maintained. This allows them to be brought back on-line in a minimal amount of time when they do go down. The future will see a movement to more computer numerically controlled (CNC) and, eventually, voice-controlled machines.

Another area that Japan sees in its future is communications technology. Japanese do not see themselves as a major leader in this area, but they are making great strides in that direction. This leadership is strongly encouraged by their lack of ability to easily transmit their Katakana or Kanji language characters via conventional computer communications technology. One area that looks promising is that of optical transmission, which avoids many of the electrical problems posed by conventional cable transmissions. Once they have overcome their own communication problems, they see the rest of the world as offering little challenge.

Japan

One more area that needs mention is Japan's immense computer manufacturing and computer development capability. The Japanese have all but stolen the world's production of computer systems by their ability to produce more efficient and cheaper equipment than their international competitors. Even giant competitors such as IBM, who are nearly impossible to drive out of the market, have been overtaken by Japan's manufacturing efficiency. Many so-called name brand computers are now produced almost entirely in Japan. The only thing that is American about them is the nameplate.

Japanese efficiency in the computer technology industry has won them a major portion of the printer and disk-drive markets. They are also major contenders for manufacturing the world's integrated circuits (ICs), such as the megabit DRAM (one million bits of dynamic random-access memory on one integrated circuit) developed by AT&T.

One last area that cannot be overlooked is Japan's intensive output of engineers. On a per capita basis, it is out-producing most of the rest of the world in the education of engineering graduates. This mass of technical ability has moved Japan from a copycat nation to one of innovation. An example of this is the lithium battery developed by Matsushita Electric which is used in the Eastman Kodak Disc Camera and offers a five-year, no replacement guarantee. It is no wonder that the rest of the high-tech countries are paying close attention to Japanese developments.

REFERENCES

Amaya, Tadashi. "The Vital Work Place: Small Group Activities In Japan," *Training And Development Journal*, Oct. 1984, pp. 31-32.

Anderson, W.S. "What We Are Learning From Japan," *Nation's Business* (March 1981), pp. 39-41.

Anonymous. "Kawasaki: Steel Uses Technology to Bolster Exports," *Business Week*, January 29, 1979, pp. 119-120.

Anonymous. "Yet Another Story On Productivity," *Journal Of American Insurance*, Fall 1981, pp. 15-19.

Asher, Shigeko M. and Ken Inoue. "Industrial Manpower Development in Japan," *Finance and Development*, September 1985, Vol. 22, #3, pp. 23-26.

Asinof, L. "A Country Cleans Up," *Science Digest*, Vol. 89, #10 (1981), pp. 76-77.

Bairstow, Jeffrey. "Automated Automaking," *High Technology*, August 1986, pp. 25-28.

_____. "Packing More Punch," *High Technology*, August 1986, pp. 29-30.

Baker, E.F. "Flow Management Can Change The Course Of U.S. Productivity Growth," *APICS 24th Annual International Conference Proceedings*, 1981, pp. 152-156.

Beal, G.L. and R.W. Evans. "Traditional P&IC Techniques And Why They Sometimes Fail: A Behavioral Approach," *APICS 22nd Annual Conference Proceedings*, 1979, pp. 17-19.

Briggs, B.B. "A Dangerous Folly Called Theory Z," *Fortune*, May 17, 1982, pp. 43-46.

Brody, Herb. "Good Is Never Enough," *High Technology*, August 1986, pp. 20-21.

_____. "Hands Across Japan," *High Technology*, August 1986, pp. 22-24.

Bromberg, H.J. "Inventory Planning—Basic Approaches That Still Apply," *Proceedings Of The 21st Annual International Conference Of APICS*, 1978, pp. 725-730.

Bryron, C. "How Japan Does It," *Time*, March 30, 1981, pp. 32-38.

Deming, W.E. "On Some Statistical Aids Toward Economic Production," *Interfaces*, Vol. 5, #4, 1975, pp. 1-15.

De Young, H. Garrett. "In Search Of A Winning Strategy," *High Technology*, August 1986, pp. 45-47.

_____. "What We Need Is A Breakthrough," *High Technology*, August 1986, pp. 43-44.

Fieleke, Norman S. "Productivity And Labor Mobility In Japan, The United Kingdom, And The United States," *New England Economic Review*, November/December 1981, pp. 27-36.

Fox, Robert E. "MRP, KANBAN, and OPT—What's Best?" *American Production and Inventory Control Society 25th Annual Conference Proceedings*, 1982, pp. 482-486.

Haavind, Robert. "Designing For Flexibility," *High Technology*, August 1986, pp. 50-52.

_____. "Moving Ahead In Communications," *High Technology*, August 1986, pp. 53-54.

_____. "Tools For Compatibility," *High Technology*, August 1986, pp. 34-42.

Hall, Robert W. *Driving The Productivity Machine*, Falls Church, Virginia: The American Production And Inventory Control Society, 1981.

_____. "Stockless Production For The United States," *American Production And Inventory Control Society 25th Annual Conference Proceedings*, 1982, pp. 314-318.

_____. "What Can Americans Copy From Japan?" *Repetitive Manufacturing Seminar Proceedings*, 1981, pp. 21-30.

Hall, R.W. and T.E. Vollman. "Black & Decker: Pioneers With MRP," *Case Studies In Materials Requirements Planning* (1978), pp. 21-47.

Harmon, Roy L. "Update 1982: U.S. Adaptation Of Japanese Techniques," *American Production And Inventory Control Society 25th Annual Conference Proceedings*, 1982, pp. 179-182.

Hatvany, N. and V. Pucik. "Japanese Management Practices And Productivity," *Organizational Dynamics*, Spring 1981, pp. 4-21.

Hayes, R.H. "Why Japanese Factories Work," *Harvard Business Review*, July-August 1981, pp. 57-74.

Hill, Arthur V. and Thomas R. Hoffman. "Manufacturing Systems Of The Future—A Delphi Study," *Production And Inventory Management*, Vol. 23, #3, 1982, pp. 87-106.

Ishii, Takemochi, Katsuto Uchihashi, Shichihei Yamamoto, Shigeru Kimura, and Masanori Moritani. *A Look At Japanese Technological Development*, 1983, Foreign Press Center, Tokyo, Japan.

Lowe, Ronald D. "Japan's Secret Weapon," *P&IM Review*, April 1985, pp. 57-58.

Nakagawa, Yatsuhiro and Nobumasa Ota. *The Japanese-Style Economic System— A New Balance Between Intervention And Freedom*, 1981, Foreign Press Center, Tokyo, Japan.

Nakane, J. and R.W. Hall. "Transferring Production Control Methods Between Japan And The United States," *APICS 24th Annual International Conference Proceedings*, 1981, pp. 192-194.

Nellemann, David O. "MRP Vs. KANBAN? Combining The Best Of The East And West," *American Production And Inventory Control Society 25th Annual Conference Proceedings*, 1982, pp. 124-128.

———. "Productivity— The Japanese Formula," *Repetitive Manufacturing Seminar Proceedings*, 1981, pp. 77-84.

Noda, M. "Business Management In Japan," *Technology Review*, Vol. 81, #7, 1979, pp. 20-30.

O'Connor, Brian J. "How Do The Japanese Get Higher Productivity Than We Do?" *American Production And Inventory Control Society 25th Annual Conference Proceedings*, 1982, pp. 477-481.

Oishi, Osamu. "Productivity And Productivity Ideas," *Business Quarterly*, Summer 1982, pp. 44-48.

Orlicky, J. *Material Requirements Planning*, New York, McGraw-Hill Book Company, 1975.

Ouchi, W.C. *Theory Z*, New York, Avon, 1982.

Pascile and Athos. *The Art Of Japanese Management*, New York, Warner Books, 1982.

Plenert, Gerhard J. "Are Japanese Production Methods Applicable In The United States?" *Production And Inventory Management*, Vol. 28, 1985.

———. *Japanese Inventory Control And Inventory Management Techniques Applicable In The United States Of America*, Sacramento, California, California State University in Sacramento, 1983.

Plossl, G.W. "Japanese Productivity: Myth Vs. Reality," *Production And Inventory Management Review*, Vol. 1, #9, 1981, pp. 59-62.

———. "MRP Yesterday, Today And Tomorrow," *Production And Inventory Management*, 1980, pp. 1-10.

Poe, Robert. "Where People Have A Place — For Now," *High Technology*, August 1986, pp. 31-33.

Posa, John G. "The Megabit RAM: Made In Japan?" *High Technology*, June 1985, pp. 37-41.

Ramsey, D. "Japan's High-Tech Challenge," *Newsweek*, August 9, 1982, pp. 48-54.

Rice, J.W. and T. Yoshikawa. "A Comparison Of KANBAN And MRP Concepts For The Control Of Repetitive Manufacturing Systems," *Production And Inventory Management Review*, Vol. 28, #1, 1982, pp. 1-15.

_____. "MRP And Motivation: What Can We Learn From Japan?" *Production And Inventory Management Review*, Vol. 21, #2, 1980, pp. 45-52.

Robinson, Richard D. "Can The Japanese Keep It Up?" *Technology Review*, August/September 1982, pp. 47-52.

Rubinger, Bruce F. "Windows On Japan," *High Technology*, August 1986, pp. 12-13.

Santora, A. "Quality Circles: When & How," *Production And Inventory Management Review*, Vol. 2, #2, 1982, pp. 20-22.

Schonberger, R.J., D. Sutton, and J. Claunch. "KANBAN (Just-In-Time) Applications At Kawasaki, USA," *APICS 24th Annual International Conference Proceedings*, 1981, pp. 188-191.

Shimomura, M. "What Makes Japan Work?" *Science Digest*, Vol. 89, #10, 1981, pp. 66-67.

Smith, L.F. and R.L. Harmon. "Closed Loop Systems In Japan: Techniques Of Worldwide Application, *APICS 24th Annual International Conference Proceedings*, 1981, pp. 105-108.

Smolens, R.W. "Design Of The Manufacturing System For The 80's," *APICS 23rd Annual Conference Proceedings*, 1980, pp. 430-432.

Stoddard, William G. "Productivity In Manufacturing: Survival Strategy For U.S. Industry," *Material Handling Engineering*, January 1985, pp. 54-64.

Wantuck, K.A. "The ABC's Of Japanese Productivity," *Production And Inventory Management Review*, Vol. 1, #9, 1981, pp. 22-27.

Weber, David E. "An Eye To The East: Training In Japan," *Training And Development Journal*, Oct. 1984, pp. 32-33.

Wight, O.W. *Production And Inventory Management In The Computer Age*, Boston: CBI Publishing Company, Inc., 1974.

Operations Research Texts

Sawaya, William J. and William C. Giauque. *Production and Operations Management*, New York: Harcourt Brace Jovanovich, 1986.

Shingo, Shigeo. *Non-Stock Production: The Shingo System for Continuous Improvement*, Cambridge, Mass.: Productivity Press, 1988.

Japan Management Association. *KANBAN Just-in-Time at TOYOTA*, Cambridge, Mass.: Productivity Press, 1986.

Karatsu, Kajime. *TQC Wisdom of Japan - Managing for Total Quality Control*, Cambridge, Mass.: Productivity Press, 1988.

Belcher Jr., John G. *Productivity Plus + How Today's Best Run Companies Are Gaining the Competitive Edge*, Houston, Tex.: Gulf Publishing Company, 1987.

7

Israel

Israel is exciting, unique, and of interest to anyone studying management styles. Israel started out with a problem that most other countries would love to have—its citizens were overeducated and overambitious for the little spot of land they owned. As a result, when Israelis needed management systems, they found it unnecessary to go to Europe or the United States for ideas; they found that they had plenty of individuals who could generate ideas. Due to the varying politics of the past two decades, Israelis found it advantageous to do their own development work.

As might be expected, Israel is behind in the labor-intensive industries. Productivity in most industries is about average when compared with Europe, but they have demonstrated some impressive management and technology advances.

In impressive management styles, several Israeli companies stand out. As an example, Israeli Aircraft Industries (IAI) has developed a reputation for being one of the most advanced in the aerospace industry, and its abilities in technological development have been described in *Aviation Week*.

Solcoor, Incorporated, is a conglomerate of some 200 plants. These include everything from electronics communications systems companies to Kibbutz cooperative factories.

In looking for areas where we can learn from Israeli experience, we find that prestrike worker sanctions are a major problem in Israel. Examples of some of the types of sanctions that often occur include:

- Refusal to work during certain periods
- Slowdowns
- Refusal to perform certain assignments

Israel

Of interest is how management reacts to these sanctions, the effect of management reactions on labor, and the effect these sanctions have on the outcome of labor negotiations. A good place to look at what is happening in Israel as a result of worker sanctions is the article by Wolkinson and Cohen referenced at the end of this chapter.

Also of interest in the area of labor-management disputes is the process of mediation. Reactions in Israel, as well as in the United States and Great Britain, have been favorable toward this process. The Krislov article cited at the end of this chapter is a good source of information on this subject.

Israel is a world leader in the diamond industry. It currently produces 80 percent of the world output in small polished stones, and has done an impressive job in both the production and marketing of these stones.

Israel has also done an impressive job of establishing itself as a leader in research and development, both in industry and agriculture. About 2.2 percent of its GNP is spent on R&D.

Israeli intelligence and ingenuity has resulted in several unique and interesting management systems. One of these is the Kibbutz system, an industrial organization developed around a communal life-style. A second management system that we will take a close look at is optimized production technology (OPT), a production scheduling technique that rivals materials requirements planning (MRP).

KIBBUTZ[1]

The Kibbutz is a small, communal organization where the united efforts of its members are meant to achieve certain production goals.[2] The production can

---

[1]Sources that will supply you with more information about the Kibbutz life-style and management system are:

Kibbutz Industries Association	Israel Aliyah Center
8 Shaul Hamelech Blvd.	870 Market Street, Suite 1047
P.O. Box 1514	San Francisco, CA 94102
Tel-Aviv 61014	
Israel	Kibbutz Alyia Desk
	27 West 20th Street
Solcoor, Incorporated	New York, NY 10011
Two Park Avenue	(212) 255-1338
New York, NY 10016	

The term *kibbutz* means "group" in Hebrew. *Kibbutzim* is the plural of kibbutz and means groups.

[2]There are actually three types of cooperative rural settlements that exist in Israel: the moshav ovdim, the moshav shitufi, and the kibbutz. However, the kibbutz has become a term used in the United States to refer to all three kinds of organizations.

Membership in the kibbutz is on an individual basis where the property is community-owned and the work and income are shared by the members. The moshav ovdim membership is by family where each family is allocated a piece of land and the efforts and rewards are by family rather than by individual. The moshav shitufi is a compromise where membership is by individual but the family maintains its own household and remuneration is by the needs of the family unit.

There are about 450 moshavim, of which 50 are structured as moshavim shitufiim and 400 are structured as moshvei ovidum.

be agricultural or industrial. It has no unions, no layoffs, and no individualized reward systems. It is built on land leased from the state and constitutes an autonomous municipal entity.

There are currently about 250 kibbutzim in Israel. Anywhere from 50 to 2,000 people reside in each one, and in all the kibbutzim represent about 2.8 percent of Israel's population. Most of the workers live in these communes, but workers are also received from other countries, such as the United States, and they visit for a set period of time. New members are given a trial period of one year and are then subject to approval and an acceptance vote by the general membership.

Industry in the kibbutzim includes such products as electronics, furniture, plastics, machinery, and many other products along with food processing facilities. In recent years, the kibbutz has undergone a process of transformation in which it has rapidly moved toward industrialization. Today, industry accounts for half of the productive output of the kibbutzim and five percent of Israel's total industrial output. Collectives of kibbutzim often ban together for marketing and trade functions.

The life-style in the kibbutz offers communal dining rooms, a laundry, medical clinics, stores, and child care. Financial security and care during disability or personal crisis receive the support of the entire community. Within the community no money is exchanged, and members of the community are given allowances for purchases outside the kibbutz.

The kibbutz life-style emphasizes family relations and builds a type of extended family. Evenings and weekends stress family ties. However, during the day, and in some kibbutzim during the night also, children are cared for in communal quarters. Women work full-time in the commune. Special arrangements are made for shorter workdays for pregnant women and for the first year after a child's birth.

Management of the kibbutz is done as a democracy with each member of the society having an equal vote at a weekly general meeting. Individual community functions such as education and housing are handled by elected committees, and executive officers for the kibbutz as a whole are also elected. Out of this environment have come many of Israel's political leaders.

Permanent work assignments are determined by the committees. Day-to-day assignments are made by a work organizer who plans each day based on the community needs. The workweek is six days, eight hours per day. Two-week annual vacations are given each worker.

Since no one is motivated to stretch out their job assignments or to work overtime, the general atmosphere fosters a search for improved working techniques and automation wherever possible. Although this life-style suggests a low cost of labor and therefore inexpensive products, the community as a whole searches for ways to improve the life-style of the general populace. Therefore, competitive pricing and cost efficiency are as important to the kibbutz as they are to any other industrial organization. The search for improved technology is an ongoing enterprise.

OPT[3]

Israel has placed a considerable amount of emphasis on the development of its industry and factories. This includes the development of software management systems for plant control. For instance, Hughes Aircraft uses an Israeli-developed production control software package.

A new production control philosophy was developed out of the need for a production control system. Rather than turn to traditional systems like MRP, the Israelis developed their own method of production control. (Economic considerations such as high inflation and poor exchange rates for the purchase of United States software products influenced this decision.) The result was optimized production technology (OPT). Now, how does OPT work and what makes it different from the traditional MRP concept of the United States?[4]

---

[3]The marketing organization for OPT in the United States is Scheduling Technology Corporation, 42 South St., Hopkinton, MA 01748, (508) 435-1001.

An excellent book on the philosophy of OPT and some of its correcting principles is *The Goal*. The book is written in storybook style and is easy reading. It can be acquired through Avraham Y. Goldratt Institute, 442 Orange St., New Haven, CT 06511, (203) 624-9026.

[4]This section will compare three systems: MRP, just-in-time production or JIT, and OPT. All three systems control production in the *discrete* manufacturing environment (one in which parts or components are fabricated and then assembled). An example is the manufacturing of engine parts and the assembly of the engine. This type of manufacturing does not include *process manufacturing*, in which the entire production process is a flow process, such as in a flour mill, an oil refinery, or a cannery. It also does not include the job shop, where items are made once and rarely again; for example, very few dental chairs are outfitted exactly alike.

These manufacturing techniques only include the discrete environment that is primarily involved in fabrication and assembly (repetitive) production but not in the assembly line (flow) production process. It is in these areas that United States industry is receiving its greatest thrashing by foreign competition.

From 1970 to 1979, inventory turnover averages were made for the United States and Japan:

Inventory Turnover Averages

	USA	JAPAN	DIFFERENCE
Job Shop	3.2	3.1	3 percent
Process	5.1	5.5	7 percent
Discrete	3.8	7.6	100 percent

Source: Robert E. Fox, "MRP, KANBAN, or OPT—What's Best?" American Production and Inventory Control Society 25th Annual International Conference Proceedings, 1982, pp. 482-486.

From this chart we can see that the major area of competitive loss is in the discrete (repetitive) manufacturing environment. This is the area in which MRP, JIT, and OPT are primarily used.

In chapter 2, we saw that the working environments in the United States, Japan, and Israel are quite different. We saw that in the United States there is no land space restriction and factories tend to be spread out. In Japan and Israel, land space is restricted and is a major production constraint.

In the United States, the major market for manufactured products is within the country. In Japan and Israel, the major markets are outside of the countries, and this makes them quality-conscious. The United States has a sales strategy that emphasizes product variability, whereas Japan restricts product options.

United States industry places emphasis on the productivity of the individual employee. This is in contrast to the Japanese and Israeli philosophy of "team productivity" or of productivity of the facility as a whole. The difference can be seen in the job-costing techniques that the United States uses. Job-costing emphasizes a standard of pieces produced per hour for each employee. This means that for employees to justify their existence, they must produce a certain number of pieces of product in a certain amount of time. This causes an employee to be concerned with individual speed rather than with overall product quality.

In the United States industrial environment, MRP systems are considered "push" systems. A list of required materials is generated in order to produce a specific number of output units. This list of materials generates purchase orders and production orders. Quite often, there are enormous scrap factors inserted into this production requirement that will generate an excess of needed materials at the purchasing end. When these materials arrive into raw materials inventory, they are pushed into the production environment based on the requirements of the MRP schedule. As each production step is completed, it pushes its output on to the next step.

In the Japanese "pull" environment, materials are not fed into the production cycle until the finished product is actually required. In other words, finished product requirements trigger production. This is much easier to do in Japan than in the United States because of the lead time for production. As a comparative example, the lead time to produce a motorcycle in the United States can be about one-and-a-half months. The production lead time for the same item in Japan would be one to two days. With such short lead times, it is much easier to start production when the finished product has been ordered. In the United States, it is necessary to build to projected forecasts, thus causing large inventories in order to satisfy anticipated requirements.

The Israeli system is a compromise of the Japanese and American methodologies. In OPT, production is not scheduled with either a "push" or "pull" philosophy. Production is scheduled on a "bottleneck" or centrally-managed basis. The bottleneck areas (see CHART 7.1) are analyzed and emphasized in production planning which is structured so that the bottleneck work centers will be utilized to the maximum. All other departments which are not bottlenecks (called nonbottlenecks; see CHART 7.2) are planned so as to keep the bottleneck departments working at full production at all times.

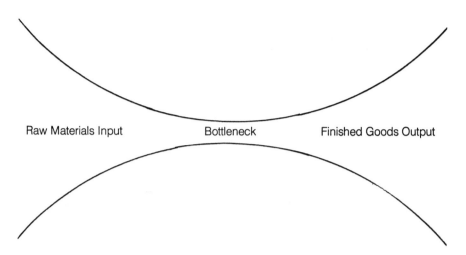

Chart 7.1. Production Flow through the Bottleneck

Raw Materials Input   Bottleneck   Finished Goods Output

The space between the lines signifies the amount of capacity in total finished units of production available at various stages in the production process. The capacity at the bottleneck is the smallest.

In CHART 7.2, the Type X work center is a bottleneck. Any reduction in set-up time adds to the total production time available, which in turn increases the total capacity output of the factory.

The Type Y work center is a nonbottleneck. In producing its share of the production necessary to match the final output of the Type X work center, the Type Y work center ends up with excess capacity, or idle time. In this case, a reduction in set-up time only causes more idle time and does not improve throughput. Production time requirements are still determined by the slowest link in the system, the bottleneck or Type X work center.

Chart 7.2. Bottlenecks vs. Nonbottlenecks

Type X Work Center		**Type Y Work Center**		
Total Time Available		Total Time Available		
Production Time	Setup Time	Production Time	Setup Time	Idle Time

When comparing OPT with the traditional MRP style of manufacturing, interesting differences appear. For example, MRP production scheduling systems sequence production tasks on the assumption that the plant has an infinite capacity available at each workstation. Afterwards, MRP attempts to adjust schedules down to realistic levels through an additional step in the production planning process. This adjusting step is called capacity requirements planning (CRP).

By requiring a two-step procedure, MRP cannot be as efficient in the development of an optimal schedule as a one-step system would be. Both JIT and OPT schedule production on the assumption of limited capacity and therefore require only one step. In JIT, the KANBAN card is used to control capacity (see the chapter on Japan) and in OPT the bottleneck is the control point which determines the plant's capacity. Additionally, OPT allows for more constraints than either the JIT or the MRP system, allowing the MRP and CRP functions to be merged into one production planning tool.

MRP systems assume that a part is passed through all stages of production in a fixed-size production batch. In reality, this does not happen. Batch sizes vary continually, and so this assumption causes computer-planned batch sizes to be larger than necessary. This is justified by the claim that the large run size will reduce set-up costs. However, attempting to constrain production to fixed-size batches imposes financial penalties on a plant.

OPT sets its priorities using the ABC concept.[5] All orders that move through a bottleneck are labeled "A" orders and are given high-priority attention, the reasoning being that you do not want to disrupt the efficiency of the bottleneck. Remember that the bottleneck determines the total throughput of the factory.

All parts that move through the bottleneck that are labeled with an "A" priority are checked more often. As we move away from the bottleneck, the production steps and orders are classified "B". Parts and orders that have no interaction with the bottleneck are labeled "C" and are given very little priority. It is assumed that the excess capacity can always make up for disruptions in the production of "C" products.

The benefit is easy to see. You only need to keep a close watch on 20 percent of your production orders in order to maximize throughput in the factory. Similarly, you only need to keep a tight control on 20 percent of your manufactured components. MRP keeps tight control on all orders and all components,

---

[5]Other names for ABC analysis are the *80-20 Rule* and the *Pareto Principle*. The concept claims that 20 percent of the orders cause 80 percent of the trouble. Similarly, 20 percent of the inventory gets 80 percent of the usage, etc. The 20 percent is labeled "A" items. The next 30 percent cause 15 percent of the problems and is called "B" items. The last 50 percent is the "C" items.

From this concept, if we pay more attention to the "A" items, we'll prevent more problems than if we give equal attention to all items. Check it out in your own factory. You'll be amazed at the consistency of this concept.

whereas under OPT, the job of plant scheduling is theoretically 20 percent of what it used to be under MRP.

Economic batch quantities (EBQ) is a concept developed by manufacturers to minimize manufacturing costs per part.[6] To achieve this goal, a balance is necessary. Any increase in the batch size reduces the amount of labor required for setting up the machines. By reducing the number of batches that are necessary, fewer setups are required. This translates into a reduced cost per part produced because setup costs are allocated across all parts.

This tendency for larger batch sizes is offset by the fact that this same increased batch size also increases the total time it takes to build a product. When more parts are produced in one batch, the total amount of time that it will take to produce a finished product will be longer. This increases financing and storage costs that translates into an increased overall cost. The balance between these two conflicting costs produces the well-known profit (cost) curve versus the batch size. The optimum is the economic batch quantity (EBQ; see CHART 7.3).

Again, JIT and OPT overcome this problem. In the case of JIT, the strategy is to reduce all setup times to a minimum. This way, setup will not be a significant factor in determining batch sizes, and batch sizes are kept small. In the OPT system, variable batch sizes are computed. OPT embodies the concept that a standardized batch size throughout the plant is unrealistic, and that even the size of the batches for the transfer of components should be different than the sizes of the batches used for production or ordering.

The excessively large batch sizes used in MRP systems encourage poor scheduling. If work centers have overlapping functions, slowness in the first center will cause start-up delays in the second center. If efficiency is being measured, the second center will appear inefficient, whereas the first can make up its delays by speeding up processing near the end of its batch. The second work center, because of its delayed start-up, will not be able to recover time lost because of these delays.

To demonstrate this, in CHART 7.4 we see a typical work schedule developed for the average worker. This is a week's worth of work, where the worker has to work 40 hours and has four jobs to do, each lasting 10 hours. As worker "A" completes his 10-hour task, he transfers job "W" to worker "B" who will also perform 10 hours of work.

Unfortunately, we do not have a plant filled with average and consistent workers. Instead, we have a plant filled with workers more like those in CHART 7.5. Here we find that employee "A" has experienced an enjoyable weekend and is not quite ready to get into the full swing of work. His first job falls a little behind schedule. So does his second job, because Tuesday is a miserable day

---

[6]Often called economic order quantity (EOQ), this concept is used to find an order size that minimizes the total inventory cost for a particular part. This is done by balancing the cost of placing an order with the cost of carrying the extra produced parts in inventory.

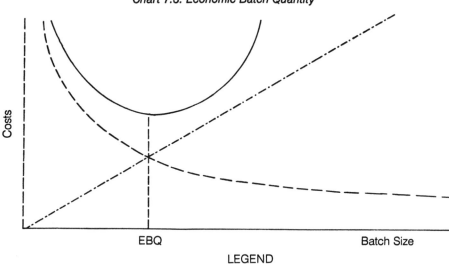

Chart 7.3. Economic Batch Quantity

<u>LEGEND</u>

—·—·—   Identifies the cost of carrying inventory which increases as the size of the batch increases.

— — —   Identifies the cost of placing the order or, in the case of production orders, the cost of the machine set-up which decreases on an average per-part basis as the size of the order increases.

———   Identifies the total cost of inventory. The lowest point on this curve identifies the desirable batch size.

too. Suddenly, he wakes up to the fact that if he doesn't get on the ball he's going to mess up his work standard by not accomplishing his four jobs in 40 hours. He successfully accomplishes all four jobs in the required amount of time. Hurrah for worker "A"! He has earned his bonus.

Now lets take a look at poor worker "B" who fits the mold as an average, consistent worker. How has "A"'s tardiness affected him? Worker "B" had to

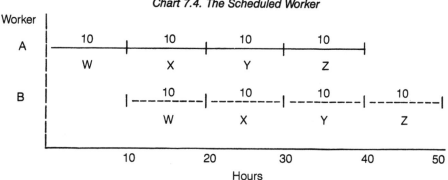

Chart 7.4. The Scheduled Worker

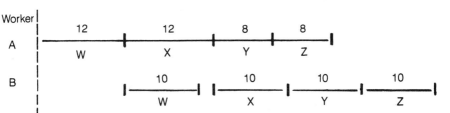

Chart 7.5. The Inconsistent Worker

start his first job two hours late, and then had another two-hour delay between the first and second job. By the time worker "B" starts job "X" he is already four hours behind on his standard, and it wasn't his fault. By the end of the week, worker "B" has missed his standard and doesn't get his bonus.

The typical solution to this problem is to give worker "B" more jobs to work on so that he'll always have something to do just in case "A" goofs off again. Unfortunately, this causes a longer lead time to produce the total product. It also increases work-in-process inventories which—at our currently high interest rates—have destroyed the competitive pricing of our products.

So how does OPT allow us to avoid the problem of worker "A" goofing off while at the same time not building up inventories? The solution is in the "Goals of OPT," which will be discussed later. The results of these goals are that we should no longer keep standards on individual employees, and if worker "B" has to wait around a little, let him wait. His waiting is cheaper than high inventories. Additionally, worker "B" should not be punished for something he could not control.

In CHART 7.1, we saw how there was more capacity available to a work center as we moved away from the bottleneck. This capacity is not potential capacity, but rather real capacity. In other words, if worker "B" is stuck with trying to do 10 hours of work in eight hours, give him some extra capacity, be it extra machines or employees, to help him achieve the 10 hours of work in eight hours. If he doesn't make it in eight hours, he affects the next employee down the line and puts him off schedule. This concept is called "safety time" wherein we should have extra *capacity* available, rather than "safety stock" with extra *inventory* available. Unfortunately, having extra people just-in-case runs against the traditional United States work ethic.

The principle of compounded delays transferred from employee "A" to employee "B" and then on to employee "C" is called "production waves." We have seen how delays are compounded as batches move through the production sequence. The result is a production wave that results in clusters of late work and clusters of idleness as we saw in the case of employee "B" (CHART 7.5).

The clusters of late work are called bottlenecks. However, these bottlenecks are labeled as "wandering" bottlenecks since they are not the same as the bottleneck defined in CHART 7.2. The wandering bottleneck is caused by the misguided scheduling of production, whereas the bottleneck in CHART 7.2 is caused by a lack of productive capacity available in the plant.

If you have ever driven near the end of a funeral procession or marched near the end of a parade, you can relate to this problem. Any delay in the line causes everyone after the delay to be affected. What you end up with is that the individuals near the front of the line drive evenly and consistently, but those at the end of the line are either rushing to catch up or standing still. Under OPT, wandering bottlenecks are inefficient and safety capacity is the solution.

In JIT, the entire production sequence is synchronized (see the chapter on Japan). A delay in one station delays work at all stations proportionately. KANBAN cards and a series of red or yellow lights are used to manage the pace of production. The production sequence is always synchronized and production waves are not allowed to occur through a similar use of safety capacity.

The goal of the traditional MRP Class "A" operation[7] is a "balanced" plant where the amount of production done at a workstation equals the amount of capacity available at that workstation. In OPT, this concept is nonsense: Production waves make it impossible to have a balanced plant since work load build-ups will continuously unbalance specific workstations. OPT favors a quantity of safety capacity available whenever possible. Only in this way can production throughput be maximized through a bottleneck, and thereby through the entire plant.

As stated several times, the performance evaluations of individuals is seen as a deterrent to productivity in the OPT philosophy. This raises the question of how performance should be evaluated. The answer to this is principally the same in both JIT and OPT. Performance is evaluated on a team basis, not on an individual basis. If team performance is evaluated rather than individual performance, and bonuses are paid based on the results of the team's performance, then the team will become the motivator of the individual. Individual motivation and evaluation is no longer a responsibility of management. Additionally, it is much easier to measure the throughput of the team rather than the throughput of individuals. (It should be stressed that throughput is measured as the number of completed products delivered to and accepted by the customer. Substandard products or made-of-stock products do not benefit the company and are not counted in the performance evaluation.)

A last key area of comparison mentioned earlier is data accuracy. In MRP, data accuracy is a critical requirement throughout the entire system. In OPT, data accuracy is only critical in the bottleneck areas and in their feeder areas. This removes most of the concern about data accuracy. Both systems require

---

[7]MRP operations are ranked as Class "A" if they satisfy a set of requirements for data accuracy (very high), customer service levels (excellent performance), and inventory levels (very low).

Traditional Financial Goals:
- Maximize net profit
- Maximize return on investment
- Maximize cash flow

Chart 7.6. The Goals for Manufacturing

OPT Operational Goals:
- Maximize throughput
- Minimize inventory
- Minimize operating expense

sophisticated computer systems to generate production schedules, but OPT typically operates faster.

In the Japanese JIT system, the need for data accuracy is almost zero, and computer systems are not needed. Production flow is managed so tightly that a computer would not produce information quickly enough to be helpful.

As previously mentioned, OPT embodies a unique set of manufacturing goals. Traditionally, the goals of manufacturing have emphasized the financial profitability of the factory (see CHART 7.6). Under OPT, though, such goals may foster some unnecessary inefficiencies in the operation of the factory. OPT claims that if the operational goals are stressed rather than the financial goals, the latter will be maximized automatically.

An example of the inefficiencies fostered by financial goals can be found in the traditional measuring techniques used for evaluating the financial month as seen in CHART 7.7. Early in the month, the cost accounting measures dominate the evaluation of production. Simply stated, since employees are evaluated on individual performance, they stress the easy, efficient jobs that will give them the highest ratings and the best bonuses.

Chart 7.7. Financial Performance Measurements

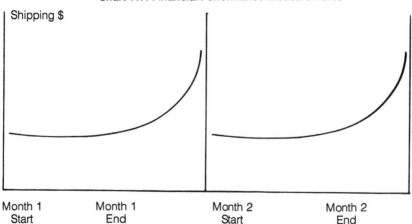

| Month 1 Start | Month 1 End | Month 2 Start | Month 2 End |

Cost accounting measures dominate the month starts and financial statement measures dominate the month ends.

Unfortunately, when the end of the month starts to roll around, financial reporting considerations take over priority. Management suddenly realizes that the company hasn't shipped enough goods in order to keep the financial statements looking good for the stockholders. A big push is then exerted to get as many goods as possible out the door, regardless of employee efficiencies. Excessive overtime and inefficient batch sizes occur in the processing of the materials.

We can see why OPT tends to avoid financial goals and stresses the operational goals of the factory. Operational goals avoid running "high performance" jobs just to make efficiencies look good and tend to keep the factory's flow of materials steady to avoid sporadic month-end pushes.

As we have seen, OPT is a totally unique way of viewing the operation of a plant. Other areas—such as job priorities, scheduling finite capacity, and sequencing jobs between departments—are handled much better with OPT. If this concept of production control interests you and you would like additional detailed information, review the literature listed at the end of this chapter. Additionally, Scheduling Technology Corporation, mentioned in footnote 3 at the start of this section, has a variety of additional detailed literature on this subject.

In converting from MRP, OPT is easier to implement than JIT. OPT can be implemented into most existing factories without a major reorganization of the machinery in the plant that is required for a JIT system. This makes OPT less disruptive to current operations, and the factory can slowly be transformed into a more efficient operation. This makes OPT appealing for those factories that need to maintain production and, at the same time, to reorganize.

SUMMARY

To summarize, OPT offers a simplification of the product scheduling process. The work required to develop and process schedules and to analyze the results from the scheduling reports has been significantly simplified. A major disadvantage of OPT is that existing information systems, such as the accounting system and the costing system, are going to be drastically changed. Due to its reduced data requirements and its move away from efficiency and performance evaluations, OPT will disrupt the information that is now considered vital in the operation of a facility. Production standard times will no longer be an effective means for managing production throughput. This change affects the accounting department, the financial analysis systems, and disrupts the users that rely on the information.

In scheduling, OPT supplies a more complete schedule than JIT, but JIT supplies a quicker schedule. MRP schedules are developed very slowly, making OPT's performance look impressive in comparison.

In considering the flexibility of the production system, JIT is by far the most flexible because of its minimal batch sizes and low inventory levels. OPT, since it also tends to schedule lower levels of inventory, and since it allows for flexible batch sizes, is a significant cost improvement over MPR.

OPT offers many of the benefits of JIT. Additionally, OPT allows for the parallel operation of the old MRP system so that the proper operation of the new OPT system can be assured prior to the dismissal of the MRP system.

In the cost of operation, data accuracy becomes a crucial consideration. Due to its high data accuracy requirements, MRP is the most costly; JIT, because of its negligible data requirements, is the cheapest. OPT, once again, falls in-between.

A complete simulation of the production process can only be realized with OPT. MRP is too complex and too time-consuming. JIT is not complete enough

Chart 7.8. OPT Advantages over Current MRP Systems

---

1) OPT offers a simplified technique for production scheduling.
   - Schedules are not as time-consuming to set up.
   - Schedules do not require as much data.
   - Less accuracy is required in the data.
   - Less computer processing capability is required.
   - Less personnel time is required to analyze the schedule.

2) The user portion of the system is not as complex as in MRP.
   - The internal mathematical technique contains additional sophistication that makes the system user's job easier.
   - User knowledge requirements are reduced.

3) Actual manufacturing resources (finite resources) are taken into account.

4) Maximization of production output and simultaneous minimization of work-in-process inventory occurs as a basis for optimization in the mathematical technique.

5) A rapid projection of the schedule occurs.
   - Quick schedules allow for the quick modification of the schedules and therefore for more flexibility in the schedules.
   - Schedule changes can occur in a few hours rather than days.
   - Quick schedule development allows for simulation to be used in the scheduling process.

6) Plant production analysis occurs.
   - Bottlenecks in the production process are specifically defined.
   - Improvements are easily made on the bottlenecks because of their clear definition.
   - Simulation can be used to test variations in plant output (product mix or load) and how this will affect the plant load.
   - Capacity changes can be simulated.

7) Ten percent or greater increases in production output using the same resources is possible.

8) Twenty percent or greater reduction in work-in-process inventory is possible.

9) Smaller batch sizes are calculated based on profitability rather than on EOQ.

10) The scheduling system allows for finite control of the resources on the short term.

Chart 7.9. OPT Disadvantages over Current MRP Systems

---

1. Plant reorganization would be required.
   - Conceptual reorganization would be required.
   - Data processing systems would be replaced.
   - Management style would need to be changed.
   - New reporting systems would need to be learned.
   - Equipment changes and movement might be necessary to facilitate using OPT efficiently.

2. OPT is more complex than JIT, which is primarily a manual system.

3. A tighter schedule is produced than in either JIT or MRP, thus allowing less ability to accommodate production errors.

4. The costing systems and accounting systems are severely disrupted.
   - Efficiency can no longer be calculated.
   - Job cost control data is restricted in some areas.
   - Performance evaluations no longer exist.

5. The financial analysis system is changed.

6. Users are disrupted.
   - Users will need to be retrained.
   - New reports will need to be developed for data processing and accounting to handle the new information base.

---

for simulation planning. CHART 7.8 offers a list of the advantages of OPT when considering MRP or JIT. CHART 7.9 shows the disadvantages of OPT.

The original developers of OPT have sold the rights to the product to Scheduling Technology Corporation. The original developers have gone on to develop what they consider to be a more advanced process of manufacturing control, which they have called Business Application Systems (BAS). This is not a software product yet; rather, it is a process or methodology of continuous improvement. Information about this process is available from the Avraham Y. Goldratt Institute. The Institute's journal, *The Theory of Constraints Journal*, explains some of these ideas in more detail.

The low productivity levels in the United States remind us that it is time for a change in our manufacturing methods. Otherwise, we have no chance of beating our foreign challengers.

REFERENCES

David, Harry I. and Denis C. LeFevre. "Finite Capacity Scheduling With OPT," *American Production And Inventory Control Society 24th Annual International Conference Proceedings*, 1981, pp. 178-181.

Fox, Robert E. "MRP, KANBAN, Or OPT—What's Best?" *American Production And Inventory Control Society 25th Annual International Conference Proceedings*, 1982, pp. 482-486.

_____. "OPT—An Answer For America—Part II," *Inventories & Production*, November/December 1982, pp. 10-19.

Goldratt, Eliyahu M. "100% Data Accuracy—Need Or Myth?" *American Production And Inventory Control Society 25th Annual International Conference Proceedings*, 1982, pp. 64-66.

_____. "Optimized Production Timetable: A Revolutionary Program For Industry," *American Production And Inventory Control Society 23rd Annual International Conference Proceedings*, 1980, pp. 172-176.

_____. "The Unbalanced Plant," *American Production And Inventory Control Society 24th Annual International Conference Proceedings*, 1981, pp. 195-199.

Goldratt, Eliyahu M. and Jeff Cox. *The Goal, Excellence in Manufacturing*, Croton-on-Hudson, New York, North River Press, Inc., 1984.

Hughes, Helen. "Capital Utilization In Manufacturing," *Finance And Development*, Vol. 20, #1, March 1983, pp. 6-9.

Krislov, Joseph. "Supplying Mediation Services In Five Countries: Some Current Problems," *Columbia Journal Of World Business*, Summer 1983, pp. 55-63.

Ministry of Foreign Affairs. Information Division, Jerusalem, *Facts About Israel*, Jerusalem, 1985.

Plenert, Gerhard J. "Are Japanese Production Methods Applicable in the United States?" *Production and Inventory Management*, Vol. 28, 1985.

_____. *Japanese Inventory Control And Inventory Management Techniques Applicable In The United States Of America*, Sacramento, California, California State University in Sacramento, 1983.

_____. "MRP, JIT, and OPT: What's 'Best'?" *Production and Inventory Management*, Vol. 27, #2, Second Quarter, 1985.

_____. *Optimized Production Technology*, Sacramento, California, California State University in Sacramento, 1983.

Stewart, Simon., "Using OPT To Schedule A Machine Shop," *American Production And Inventory Control Society 25th Annual International Conference Proceedings*, 1982, pp. 92-93.

Wolkinson, Benjamin W. and Abraham Cohen. "Use Of Work Sanctions In Israeli Labour Disputes," *British Journal Of Industrial Relations*, Vol. 20, #2, July 1982, pp. 231-246.

8

Asia's New Strength

Japan is the shining industrial star of Asia. It has advanced from a destroyed, chaotic country after World War II to Asia's industrial giant. The rest of Asia has watched this process carefully and is now saying, "Why not us?" Many countries are struggling to learn Japan's industrial management techniques, and they are learning fast. Additionally, the cost of labor is cheaper in many of these other countries than it is in Japan. The hope of Asia is to use Japanese production techniques which are cost efficient, and then to undersell the Japanese in their own markets.

Four "tigers" have emerged in Asia that have made significant inroads into Japanese markets: Hong Kong, Taiwan, Singapore, and South Korea. These countries have all emerged from a status of less developed countries (LDCs) to one of new industrial countries (NICs). It was Japan's role 10 to 15 years ago to be the Asian copycat of United States technology, and this role was then taken over by these four tigers. However, they are now emerging from this role and are beginning to develop their own products and services. They are all expressing a new commitment to entrepreneurship. They plan to combine their own resources with what they have learned overseas. It will be interesting to watch their continued rapid growth and industrialization.

It will also be important to watch the powerhouse of development that is taking place in the PRC (People's Republic of China). Although most observers do not yet consider the PRC a major industrial threat, most conclude it is a matter of time before the country takes advantage of its enormous population and takes an industrial lead in Asia.

The process that is unfolding is both interesting and educational. The new industrializing Asian countries want to take a piece of Japan's market away by advancing into high technology quickly. Management in Asia has also stepped into a new era of motivation and organization. We will look at just a few examples of what is happening in Asia to see what we can learn.

CHINA

China has played a suppressed and hidden role for a millennium. Only recently has it emerged as a nation interested in the economic growth and development experienced by the Western nations. However, in spite of the new-found interest, the Chinese are trying to maintain their traditional moral and ethical ideals. The governmental structure of the People's Republic of China (PRC) is that of communistic one-party rule and acts as a highly centralized decision-making force that directly affects the life-styles of every individual.

Communist communes have been developed throughout the country, managed primarily by a communist party hierarchy. The communistic motivation-oriented programs parallel the religious revival groups of the United States in their attempt to generate an audience of believers. Approximately 75 percent of the labor force is employed in agriculture primarily in this type of environment.

This communistic structure has, to some extent, overlayed religious philosophy, but undercurrents of traditional religion still hold tight in many ways. For example, strong, clanlike family ties persist and remain as a dominating influence in the lives of the people.

Many "plans" have been established, all in an attempt to motivate the population. Recently, incentive systems were established so that a worker can receive as much as 50 percent of his base pay in a bonus. The new philosophy emphasizes that each worker should receive compensation according to his labor, a drastic change from the traditional communistic work ethic.

Fringe benefits have also become popular. Some examples include lifetime employment, complete disability, paid sick leave, full medical care, generous retirements, family support in the event of death, meal halls, children's education, day care centers, and employee loans.

Many factories have established quota systems wherein the employees can receive bonuses for surpassing quotas. Additionally, the factory receives some of the financial benefit of surpassed quotas, and management is allowed to invest this money in ways that will benefit the factory and its employees. The government still dominates the centrally-planned economy, but some autonomy is now being allowed at the factory level, especially if quotas are exceeded.

On the other half of the economic pie, as companies increase their throughput, the consumers of the nation will need to consume more. This means that China will need to rethink its centrally-managed pricing structure.

Industry currently shows a great deal of backwardness. At the same time, we see that a great deal of potential development exists due to the vast resources that are available. Foreign investment is now being encouraged.

Unions exist but are very different than their U.S. counterparts. Unions work for the government, and there is often some question of whether their interests are more oriented to the government or the workers. Chinese trade unions follow the same pattern as other communistic trade unions. They transmit the party line, encourage production, engage in political and ideological education, oversee safety and sanitation, and handle welfare and cultural responsibilities. About 95 percent of all employees are members of the unions, but this percentage is decreasing as ideologies are changing.

The recruitment, selection, and placement of personnel is very similar to the methods used in the United States. Applications are made, individuals are interviewed and tested, and selections are made. Adherence to the political party line is not as strong a factor as may be thought. The high unemployment rate motivates "job creation" programs by the government where employees are used less than efficiently, and this unfortunately builds in a tolerance of substandard performance.

The concept of the "worker-controlled enterprise" allows employees to have a strong say as to who will be promoted to supervisory levels of management. This process is not under the sole control of management. The selection process involves a form of worker interview wherein worker input into the selection process is requested.

Lateral transfers between or within companies are rare. All companies must conform to the same set of centrally-determined labor plans. Releases from previous employers are required before a new job can be started, and productive workers are rarely released.

Training is vital, but training programs are allocated under the discretion of a selection committee made up of management, employees, and the union. The party influence is not strong. (During visits to the PRC, interpreters openly suggested when the information being relayed was factual or along "party lines.")

A "workers congress" is a representative organization for a company's workers. About one representative for every 10 to 15 workers sits on the congress. This group is established to administer budgets, do production planning, supervise research and development, make decisions on wages and benefits, administer discipline, and plan administrative procedures. The congress works with management to establish those measures and works for efficiency and productivity improvements.

In the move toward industrial democracy, the roles of the unions, workers congresses, and management have shifted considerably in some plants. Specific roles are no longer consistent between plants. However, the workers congresses and the trade unions are consistently involved in the selection of supervisory personnel.

In summary, recent economic reforms have promoted:

1. Bonus incentive systems
2. Reforms in industrial management
3. The replacement of budget allocations with bank loans

4. "Profit" taxes for industry to the state
5. Private enterprise expansion
6. "Free markets" to be established in the cities
7. A liberalized distribution system
8. A dismantling of the commune system

Trade promotion conferences are being established in China in order to open the door to technology. The Chinese realize that importing high-tech equipment is essential to their technological reform. Information about the transfer of technology to China is available from:

U.S. Export Development Office
7th Floor, World Import Mart
1-3, Higashi Ikebukuro, 3-Chome
Toshima-ku, Tokyo, Japan
Telephone: 987 2441
Telex: 2722446

China offers an enormous market for United States producers of goods and technology. It also offers an open door for Westerners to become involved in the modernization of an enormous culture. To receive additional information about the commercial opportunities in China contact:

U.S. Department of Commerce
International Trade Administration
Office of PRC and Hong Kong, H2317
Washington, D.C. 20230
Telephone: (202) 377-3583

Lewis Lehr, Chairman and Chief Executive Officer of 3M Corporation, is quoted as having said: "If the Western World thinks Japan has been a problem, wait until those 1.2 billion Chinese start producing TV sets and radios." 3M is working with the People's Republic of China to open a manufacturing plant in Shanghai that will produce tapes, resins, and connectors for that nation's communications and power services. Lehr sees the U.S. government and business forming a close relationship with this potentially tremendous market.

Technological advancement is primarily hampered by the ability of management to adapt to the new tools available to them. The PRC has invested in computers and various other forms of technology, only to find that their management personnel were not ready for this type of technology. The result is that, in the future, training programs and a thorough understanding of technology will be mandatory for such purchases.

China emphasizes training and the transfer of technology as a contractual part of any commercial negotiations. For example, in the development of China's oil resources, the Offshore Petroleum Regulations clearly state that the foreign contractor "is obliged to transfer the technology and pass on the experience to the personnel of China." Many commercial entrants take this obligation lightly and find out that China expects a significant financial outlay to assure the adequate transfer of the technology. Further information on this is available in the article by Burns cited at the end of this chapter.

A substantial amount of good information exists about doing business in China. I recommend two sources. One is the magazine *The China Business Review* which had a good article by Dennis B. Keley. The other is the book *Foreign Trade, Investment and the Law in the People's Republic of China* by A.J. Moser. The complete references for both are at the end of this chapter.

Another inroad into China that many businesses are banking on is through Hong Kong. China's takeover in 1997 is viewed by many as the door that will allow them to enter China and automatically become part of its business environment. Factories and industries that are not receiving acceptance in the PRC hope that the Hong Kong connection will be their road to future success.

The management lessons we can learn from the PRC are many. For example, the techniques used by the government of China to change the mindsets of large masses of people are interesting. Additionally, their approach to workplace democracy is unique. However, the most important lesson to be learned from the PRC is still in the future—the change of a management philosophy from communistic to capitalistic.

For U.S. managers, there are several lessons to be learned from the PRC. Its growing development of worker-managed enterprises is an area where they are passing us by. However, the more important reason for including the PRC in this book is based on the second and third tools to help managers become more competitive, as stated in chapter 1. The first requires that the U.S. manager must have a better understanding of foreign competitors. Since the PRC will soon become the strongest manufacturing and marketing force in Asia, it should be watched and understood. The second encourages the manager to "internationalize," and a better understanding of the PRC is one of the keys to future international markets.

HONG KONG

Hong Kong is planning for its pending turnover to the PRC in 1997 when its lease with Great Britain ends. In planning for this takeover, many businesses are moving to Hong Kong in hopes that their foothold will open up the entire PRC market to them after the takeover. Additionally, many Chinese businesses are moving out of Hong Kong as a result of fear and apprehension. They aren't really sure what the takeover means to them, and they want to stay safely away from any chance of becoming nationalized.

Hong Kong is already working closely with the PRC. For example, Hong Kong designs software systems for which workers in the PRC write programs.

Another example is that Hong Kong is used as a staging area where small plants are set up. Once these are working efficiently, much larger versions are constructed in China, again taking advantage of the large, inexpensive labor force. In this way, Hong Kong takes advantage of the one-fifth labor rates of the PRC. In turn, the PRC is learning and preparing to become competitive in the international marketplace.

Although most Hong Kong-PRC ventures currently emphasize medium-level technology (labor-intensive areas), the hope is that the PRC will soon become a partner in high-tech transfers as well. These transfers will be lucrative for both sides even though the PRC requires 25 percent of the profits to be paid to them. However, the requirement that all plants built in China must be turned over to the government in 15 to 25 years (depending on the type of factory) restricts the types of joint ventures that are tried.

Hong Kong investors are optimistic, claiming that in 15 years the technology will be obsolete anyway. Their hope is that by the time the PRC takes over their plants, they'll be ready to build new ones and repeat the cycle.

In the manufacturing industry, Hong Kong has found its own niche in being able to produce products that are "hot," and as soon as larger producers latch on to the products, the Hong Kong producers move on to other "hot" products. They have the unique ability to make quick and radical changes to their product lines. They are much more efficient at product line changeovers than any of their competitors, including the United States. They cater to fad markets such as Cabbage Patch Dolls and Transformers.

In Hong Kong, unlike the majority of its neighbors, we find no government support of industry. There is no industrial targeting and no support of industries in trouble. If a company gets in trouble, it dies. Still, Hong Kong sees its future as thriving in industries such as:

- Advanced automation
- Precision manufacturing
- Computer-aided design (CAD)
- Computer-aided manufacturing (CAM)

Hong Kong sees the increase in automation as a threat to its industrial strength. It feels that, with this automation, many plants will return to Japan, the United States, and Europe. Therefore, Hong Kong views itself as playing the role of a major trading center and as a center of communications and banking, and hopes to be the centerpoint of activity for all of the PRC.

For the United States manager, Hong Kong offers an interesting lesson of adaptability. Its ability to quickly adapt manufacturing processes to market changes allows it to be a leader in the manufacture of new products, this in spite of its long distance from the American continent. With the advanced technological capability of the United States, we should be able to become more adaptable and recapture the leading-edge markets.

Hong Kong's use of plant staging should also be of interest to the international manager. It suggests that plants could also be staged in the United States before they are transferred overseas in order to make the transfer as smooth as possible.

INDIA

India is a nation of extremes. Its wealth is highly polarized and its industry is either ancient or very modern. Additionally, India's culture is in conflict with its trend toward industrialization. Long before Ghandi, the Hindu personality developed a passive resistance to development and industrialization because this was always associated with foreign domination. Now, after hundreds of years of this domination, India is independent and attempting to industrialize.

The government of India has set ambitious goals to reduce unemployment and to increase the living standard of the nation's poor. Unfortunately, new government policies that inhibit foreign investment make business in any form difficult, but conditions are slowly changing since the pressures for an improved national economy are strong.

What makes India interesting to a student of management effectiveness is its steady progress, this in spite of overwhelming problems of cultural resistance to change and the enormous population. Perhaps we can learn something of how cultures facing these challenges can still persist in international development and growth.

India has a mixed economy, with agriculture comprising 49 percent of the nation's output. Indians have an autocratic family structure, which develops a strong degree of family allegiance in any disagreements regarding development or growth. This has facilitated a technique of worker participation which uses shop and joint worker councils which may also show promise for the United States.

India's management style requires a leader who is liked and respected by the workers. If he is, the employees work with a positive motivated effort. Unfortunately, if the manager is not respected, then neither is the employee's work. The entire worker-job relationship is dependent on the employer-employee relationship.

In India, personalized relationships are much more important than contractualized relationships. An effective boss earns his subordinate's respect by offering support for the employee's work, personal, and social needs. A good manager is one who is committed to the growth of his employees. This then is in turn contingent upon the subordinate's task accomplishment. What develops is a strong relationship based on an understanding of each other's needs which in the end tends to lead to higher productivity.

The technique of employee-management relations evolves through a series of stages:

1. During the initial stages of employment, employees lean heavily on the leader for guidance, direction, support, and encouragement.

2. The employees develop skill and experience and gain self-confidence. They start to enjoy their work and to assume greater responsibilities. In turn, they need less direction.
3. When the employees start to mature in their jobs, they develop a commitment to it. They now strive for recognition and an influence and participation in the decision-making process. The manager, in turn, reduces the level of guidance and direction he gives the employees but maintains his warm relationship with them.
4. The employees become encouraged by their growth and feel a greater value to the company. This encourages them to be even more productive.
5. Eventually, both manager and employees have worked themselves into a participative system in which they all participate fully and freely in the decision-making process. Their personalized relationship never deteriorates during this entire process.

This entire process is interesting in that it starts at a lower level than most employer-employee relationships. It starts at the human relationship level and grows to a much higher level than most relationships are allowed to grow. This relationship develops to the point where distinctions between employee and employer are minimized. The leader (manager) becomes the group's representative to outsiders such as higher levels of management, vendors, or customers. The members of the group run the group with the full involvement of everyone, including the leader.

This process does not always bring success because it takes a special type of manager who can be a domineering "guiding light" at one time and then change hats to become a participative manager at another time. However, given the appropriate type of leader, the process is very successful.

Examples of management effectiveness can be seen by annual labor productivity increases in the following areas:

- Steel production
- General engineering
- Nonelectrical machinery
- Cotton spinning and weaving

India has developed a program in Gujarat that is oriented towards identifying and training entrepreneurs. This program was developed by the financial institutions of the city and is called the Entrepreneurship Development Program (EDP) which believes that potential entrepreneurs can be identified and that their latent talents can be tapped. The program integrates instruction and counseling and builds on the actual operation of an enterprise.

EDP uses psychological-behavioral testing and personal interviews to identify potential entrepreneurs, and then initiates a program of careful guidance toward suitable enterprises and sets up appropriate training programs. Training includes hands-on experience and is designed to motivate participants. The training program lasts 150 hours which are flexibly arranged to meet the participants' schedule.

EDP sees its role as operational rather than academic training. It attempts to strengthen confidence in the individual's ability and to impart necessary skills and knowledge. It provides financial, technical, and managerial business training. It also provides information and assistance in identifying and implementing projects, and then provides financial and technical assistance to begin these projects.

EDP keeps costs down by drawing volunteers from established businessmen and entrepreneurs who participate at their own cost. Using these individuals also keeps the program tailored and practical. The program has no full-time faculty other than a trainer-motivator who provides the backbone and structure of the program. Most of the actual training is provided by the volunteer managers and executives.

As a follow-up program, newly formed businesses started by these entrepreneurs are visited by EDP to identify and resolve operational problems. Its staff of volunteers provide this valuable assistance.

As a result of the success of EDP, 50 agencies in 20 states have started similar programs. Even though these new programs are not as developed as EDP, they are being assisted in that direction by EDP and will eventually become a major force in India's industrial growth.

To date, 60 percent of the participants have successfully started new businesses, of which 75 percent have been profitable. However, the success is much broader than these numbers indicate since new jobs have been created along with new opportunities for growth.

This program has had far-reaching effects in the remote areas of India. Participants have been drawn from these areas and have returned to set up new businesses. EDP has opened the door for participants from a variety of experienced backgrounds including farmers, traders, and the unemployed.

A similar program called the Training and Visit (T&V) system is sponsored by the World Bank. In this program, extension agents travel to remote, rural locations to share technological information and ideas. This seems to be the only way to inform and educate the farmers. This program has also met with considerable success.

Although remote and containing a culture far removed from our own, India offers some valuable lessons for both United States businesses and for newly developing countries trying to learn from the successes of others.

SOUTH KOREA

South Korea has come to be known as the "Economic Miracle" of Asia. In 1962, its per capita gross national product was $80, and by 1986 it climbed to

$2,300. It still has a long way to go in order to catch up with the United States, but with the astounding growth it has experienced so far, it shouldn't be long before it catches up.

South Korea has been a very attentive student, learning as much as possible from its Japanese neighbor about manufacturing. Its effect will soon be noticed in the automobile and electronics industries. South Korea plans to rank as one of the top 10 producers in each of the following areas:

- Shipbuilding (already there)
- Electronics (already there in some products like televisions)
- Automobiles
- Steel
- Petrochemicals
- Cement

Internally, South Korea has shown the signs of an economic boom. More and more people are being employed by the new industrial sectors. The major trading organizations of Hyundai and Daewoo are optimistic about the economic surge they believe is soon to come. In shipbuilding, Korea already ranks second only to Japan. In television, it ranks fourth but is a growing challenger.

Government planners have targeted microelectronics, telecommunications, new materials, automobiles, and pharmaceuticals as the five most important growth industries for South Korea. Since this country is politically very structured, industry tends to follow the suggestions of its government.

The government connection is very strong. Corporate officials meet regularly with government planning officials to discuss the goals of the nation. Corporations work towards these goals, and in return they get various forms of protectionism and the assurance that capital loans will be made available by the Korea Development Bank which funds new ventures.

Korean business is dominated by five major conglomerates which all have close ties to the government. These are Daewoo, Hyundai, Lucky-Goldstar, Samsung, and Sunkyong. These companies earn more than half of the nation's GNP and employ nearly one-half million people. Additionally, South Korea has massive trading houses similar to those found in Japan which are not hampered by antitrust regulations and are active in international trade, insurance, banking, securities, and tourism.

South Koreans have earned the attention of many nations. They do not have the high wages of Japan or the United States and this allows them to build the Japanese product using Japanese technology at a lower-than-Japanese wage rate. Soon, the United States and other world consumers will recognize and take advantage of South Korea's lower-cost products, much to the frustration of their Japanese teacher.

South Korea is one of the world's four largest debtor nations. However, unlike the other three, it has used this debt to establish an asset base. South

Korea has used the funds it has borrowed to create new industries and to strengthen existing, growing industries. From these stronger industries, a series of internationally competitive industries has emerged.

In Korea we find protectionism of small infant industries that have been targeted for growth. This allows the industry to develop within the country to the point where it will eventually become an international competitor. Most of the industries with this special brand of protectionism are selected because of their future export potential. A special government agency has been established to provide venture capital loans to small- and medium-sized businesses; this helps to support current businesses and assists in the development of many new enterprises.

Lucky-Goldstar Group controls 40 percent of South Korea's video cassette recorder market, 45 percent of its color television market, and 46 percent of its microwave market. The company is a conglomerate with businesses ranging from oil refining to stock brokering.

What is even more impressive about this organization is its drive. Lucky-Goldstar has jumped into a technological revolution, investing ever-increasing amounts of money into technology in order to become technologically independent. In spite of doubling its R&D expenditures in the last few years, it is only beginning to get close to Japanese R&D expenditures, but the push has begun.

Within Korea, three other major conglomerates are taking strides to follow the Lucky-Goldstar lead. The Samsung conglomerate is already becoming a major threat to the heavy electronics R&D emphasis of Lucky-Goldstar, followed by Daewoo and Hyundai.

The most crucial problem facing this technological surge is the need to find skilled employees that can work in the R&D areas. This is complicated to some degree by the strong nepotism that exists within Korean companies. Lucky-Goldstar is trying to circumvent this problem with an extensive recruiting program that searches for Koreans working abroad. These individuals are then targeted and efforts are made to entice them to return to Korea to work. This program has been fairly successful, and we now find many naturalized United States citizens working in the management ranks of this conglomerate.

South Korean companies are concerned about the reluctance of the Japanese to teach them since Japan sees Korea as a competitor. Korea has increased internal R&D development projects, but because of the difficulty in staffing R&D teams, some Korean companies expect future hardships caused by the Japanese pull-out. This has inspired many companies to establish links with the United States in the hope that the technological flow can be maintained. For example, Lucky-Goldstar has established links with Honeywell Information Systems and AT&T.

Another technique for acquiring technology is to establish and operate a production facility in the United States. This offers the Koreans the opportunity to learn from individuals that are considered technological experts in the field. Lucky-Goldstar was the first Korean company to establish a plant in the United

States when it built a television manufacturing facility in Huntsville, Alabama. This plant has been so successful that production volume has nearly quadrupled. Lucky-Goldstar has started producing microwave ovens in a nearby facility.

South Korea has demonstrated that the mastery of all types of technology is not necessary for industrial development. In its case, experience with production engineering has been sufficient to make it an industrial leader. In Korea we see the ability to choose a form of technology that is best suited for its industry long before it has mastered the technology.

Lucky-Goldstar is a shining star in South Korea's growth. From it we can learn several important lessons. The first is the need for a strong relationship between education and technological development; its support of R&D training programs and of education shows this. Lucky-Goldstar has the strong promotion of export markets as a goal for success, and this is strengthened by the government's targeting of specific industries. A last key element of its success is that it constantly strives for technological maturity which it hopes will someday make it a leader rather than a follower.

Similar trends can be found in the other conglomerates. For example, Daewoo Telecom reinvests 10 percent of its revenues into research and the development of new products. Its emphasis is on fiber optics and IBM-compatible personal computers. Similarly, Samsung Electronics Company (SEC) is returning nine percent of its revenues into research and development.

There is never success without trials, though. In the case of South Korea, the trials come in two forms. The first is a very authoritarian government. Korean industry has learned to work effectively with this government. However, student and labor activists hold frequent and often violent demonstrations that push for full democracy, and this instills a climate of turmoil within the nation.

The second trial is North Korea with the world's seventh largest army. The South feels that the North poses a major threat of invasion, and this forces it to invest six percent of its GNP into national defense.

In spite of many trials and challenges, South Korea is working towards future growth. Its level of effort cannot be equal to that of the Japanese or the United States. South Koreans work 10 hour shifts, six days a week. They want to catch up and eventually move ahead of the West. They recognize that they must work harder and longer to do so.

TAIWAN

When comparing the PRC with Taiwan, it's hard to believe that the people of both stem from the same ancestors. In the PRC we find communism and socialism strongly influencing life-styles, and in Taiwan we find capitalism and Confucianism as the major influences.

Confucius supported a doctrine of social harmony. In the Taiwanese workplace, the relationship between worker and employee is more important than the amount of work that is done. In fact, this becomes an important factor in performance appraisals.

Performance measures include rating scales that consider social harmony and a corporate paternalism. In general, five principles of management practice are used for evaluation, and these are taken from the Confucius doctrine that life should be organized into five relationships. These are (the first role represents leaders and the second servants or subjects):

1. Emperor-subject
2. Father (teacher)-son (student)
3. Husband-wife
4. Older brother-younger brother
5. Senior friend-junior friend

These role definitions are used in establishing the guidelines for performance appraisals, treating the business as a family with the CEO as an emperor.

This relationship places a great deal of responsibility upon the superior member. He is responsible for all the actions of his subordinates. In order to save "face," the superior will often suppress writing critical evaluations that someone else may see.

The reward system emphasizes social recognition from top management. In order to receive this recognition, problems or failures are often hidden. The internal organizations compete with one another for this recognition and everyone wants to look as good as possible in their relationships.

Individual performance appraisals include such factors as an employee's ability to budget himself within his means, gender (women are subservient), and sicknesses at home. Interdependence and the ability to work with others is placed above independence and individual achievement.

The appraisal process also includes annual activity reports in the form of essays. These outline the year's accomplishments and the coming year's plans. There is no reference to past mistakes or shortcomings. Rather, the reports are designed to show an expression of social harmony and the ability for consensus decision-making. An employee soon learns to read between the lines in looking for things that were left out of an appraisal; for example, no bonus and no salary increase means a poor rating.

Individuals are rarely fired, since this amounts to the "abandonment of a child" and is the admission of the failure of a "good father" who should teach his "child" proper principles. Rather, poor performers are transferred to other departments.

The importance of the employer-employee relationship in Taiwan is markedly different in the United States. Although the Taiwanese approach may seem extreme, it has lessons for us to learn about how to deal with others in close working relationships. We should recognize that we are very informal about a relationship that is extremely important to some other cultures.

In industry, Taiwan has found itself plagued with poor labor efficiency and excessive amounts of inventory, and these cannot be covered by low labor costs for too much longer. Goals are now focused on automation on both the factory floor and in production management methodologies. The Taiwan government is offering tax rebates for companies that invest in efficiency-increasing technologies.

Taiwan cashes in on its low labor costs which are the result of a largely unskilled labor force, but recent pressures from Malaysia and the Philippines have caused the loss of many jobs. This forced Taiwan to realize that a change was necessary, and this involves advanced technology. Many companies are starting to design and produce their own products. They no longer want to be a manufacturing colony for the United States and Japan.

Taiwan has turned to producing large quantities of transistors, printed circuit boards, and computer terminals. Major industrial parks are being planned and established in close proximity to universities in the hope that a synergistic effect will result. The emphasis in these parks is on R&D in the hope that Taiwan will develop its own technological base.

Government laboratories have been established in an attempt to apply resources to product innovation. The result is many developments in integrated circuits which are being sold internationally.

A list of governmental industrial priorities include:

- Information processing (computers, telecommunications)
- Precision machinery (factory automation)
- Materials science (electronics materials)
- Biotechnology
- Optoelectronics
- Energy

Also high on the list of expenditures is national defense. One-half of the government's R&D expenditures fall into this category. This stems from the government's constant fear of takeover by the communists.

Taiwan still faces the problem of increasing its talent pool, and to this end it needs to expand its educational facilities. There are always more applicants than openings in the universities. Taiwan is also trying to draw back many of the nationals that have left the country for better jobs or a better education overseas, but the effort is difficult since the living standard is very low compared to Western standards.

In spite of these struggles, Taiwan flourishes with entrepreneurs and boasts some 38,000 independent companies, most of which are family operations. These are evidence of the enormous potential and drive of the Chinese people who, given the proper educational and industrial opportunities, push themselves forward. They quickly adjust to technological changes and can readily adapt to new product lines.

Taiwan wants to compete with Korea's Samsung electrical complex, but currently does not have any companies of sufficient size or strength to do so. Most businesses are small, family-run operations, and it is difficult to unite them. They will thus never achieve the strength of Samsung. The hope is that governmental support will help to structure Taiwan so as to accomplish this goal.

To the benefit of the Taiwanese, we find a problem that most countries wish they had. Here we have a rich government with more money than it can figure out how to spend. This results from an enormous trade surplus. The government uses this to provide generous incentives, such as supporting 49 percent of the start-up costs of a business targeting a strategic technology. The government also supports 25 percent of the ownership, leaving the entrepreneur in need of only 26 percent of the costs of starting a business. Tariff exemptions are given for the purchase of manufacturing equipment, and various tax plans and incentives are offered the new company. Protectionism is also used to help the new company develop markets internal to the country.

Sadly, Taiwan still has the appearance of a developing country. It has a reputation for inferior goods, this primarily due to a low regard for quality. Still, Taiwan is a nation of free-thinkers and is not at all comparable to the Japanese consensus management mentality. This is evident in the large number of small businesses and in the individual drive for advancement that is characteristic of the Chinese.

For further information on production and marketing in Taiwan contact:

China Productivity Center
11th Floor, 201-26
Tun Hua N. Road
Taipei, Taiwan (105)
Republic of China

SOME OTHER COUNTRIES

Asia is a powerhouse of rapidly developing countries. We Westerners tend to lump them into a group and think of them as being very similar. However, Japan is no more like China than the United States is like Mexico. The variety and diversity of the different cultures is enormous, and so is the speed at which they are developing. Their levels of development also differ dramatically. A list of a few, but by no means all, of the countries worth studying includes:

- Indonesia
  Indonesian Embassy
  2020 Massachusetts Ave., NW
  Washington, DC 20036

- Malaysia
  Malaysian Embassy
  2401 Massachusetts Ave., NW
  Washington, DC 20008
- The Philippines
  Philippine Chamber of Commerce and Industry (PCCI)
  Chamber of Commerce Building
  Magallanes Street
  Port Area
  Manila, Philippines
- Thailand
  Office of Commercial Counselor
  Royal Thai Embassy
  1990 M Street, NW, Suite 380
  Washington, DC 20036

As was stated previously, the "four tigers"—sometimes referred to as the "four dragons"—of the Orient are Hong Kong, Singapore, South Korea, and Taiwan. These are the four strong growth nations that businesses are closely watching. Their common traits are their fast growth and relationship-oriented management philosophies. Relationship-oriented performance appraisal, as mentioned in the section on Taiwan, is also common for these countries.

Each of the four tigers has its own special flair for development. Taiwan has a strong, favorable balance of trade, while South Korea and Singapore have deficits in this area. All boast growing per capita gross national products and increasing imports. Some are very modern by Western standards, like Singapore, while others still appear underdeveloped. Each is unique in the way it manages its enterprises, and each sees the others as competitors.

Singapore is often considered the outstanding success story of Southeast Asia. In two decades, it was able to elevate itself from the level of a developing country to a standard of living comparable with the Western world. This rapid development has brought Singapore to the forefront of industrialization and has made it a competitive giant.

Unfortunately, this growth has taken its toll on the country. Singapore has lost its labor-cost advantage and is also facing stiff competition from the other three tigers. All of this, in combination with the downturn of the petrochemical market, has resulted in a recession in a once-booming economy that boasted annual growth rates of 8 to 15 percent.

Singapore has taken steps to increase R&D funding, but its investment in this area is still far behind that of the United States or its other Asian neighbors. Plans for the future include the development of advanced technology.

Singapore remains highly dependent on other countries to bring in and develop much of its own technology. It entices companies to develop in Singapore with incentives that include:

- Several years of tax-free profits
- R&D assistance programs
- Product development assistance programs
- Programs to reduce start-up and training costs
- Science parks that offer low rental rates, consulting services, short start-up times, research grants

For additional information on marketing and management in Singapore contact:

Embassy of Singapore
1824 R St., NW
Washington, D.C. 20009

SUMMARY

In industry, Asia is the present and the future. Countries like Japan, Singapore, Hong Kong, and South Korea are quickly dominating many industries that were previously dominated by Westerners. Within Asia also lies the next wave of industry-dominating countries, such as the Peoples Republic of China, Taiwan, India, Malaysia, and Indonesia.

We can learn many lessons from the growth of these Asian nations. For example, most have a unity between government, unions, and industry that allows them to target specific industries with a nationalistic effort. They are also more responsive and adaptive to market changes and can perform quick changeovers in their production processes. Their strong push for technological growth is more intense than in almost any other nation of the world.

We should take advantage of our technological potential and become a part of the rapid growth that Asia is experiencing. Programs such as India's entrepreneurship program could help rekindle the fires of growth for United States businesses. For more information, contact the departments whose addresses are listed in this book and review the articles cited at the end of this chapter.

REFERENCES

Anonymous. "China Adjusts Development Strategy," *Business America*, Nov. 26, 1984, Vol. 7, #24, pp. 2-10.

Anonymous. "Malaysia—Sustained Growth Into The Next Decade Is Anticipated; U.S. Exporters In Improved Position To Win Major Sales," *Business America*, Sept. 10, 1979, Vol. 2, #19, pp, 24-25.

Anonymous. *The World Bank Research News*, Spring 1983, Vol. 4, #1, pp. 20-23.

Bairstow, Jeffrey. "South Korea: Giants Drive Development," *High Technology*, Nov. 1986, Vol. 6, #11, pp. 20-23.

Bell, Martin, Bruce Ross-Larson, and Larry E. Westphal. *Assessing The Performance Of Infant Industries*, World Bank Staff Working Papers, No. 666, September 1984.

Bhatt, V. "Entrepreneurship Development: India's Experience," *Finance And Development*, March 1986, Vol. 23, #1, pp. 48-49.

Brody, Herb. "Taiwan: From Imitation To Innovation," *High Technology*, Nov. 1986, Vol. 6, #11, pp. 24-27.

Burns, Sandra K. "When Training Is The Law," *Training And Development Journal*, Oct. 1984, Vol. 38, #10, pp. 29-31.

Covey, Roger E. "Manufacturing In The Far East," *P&IM Review*, Oct. 1986, Vol. 6, #10, pp. 37-38.

Dahlman, Carl J., Bruce Ross-Larson, and Larry E. Westphal. *Managing Technological Development—Lessons From Newly Industrializing Countries*, World Bank Staff Working Papers, No. 717, January 1985.

Dahlman, Carl J., and Francisco C. Sercovich. *Local Development And Exports Of Technology—The Comparative Advantage Of Argentina, Brazil, India, The Republic Of Korea, And Mexico*, World Bank Staff Working Papers, No. 667, September 1984.

Dahlman, Carl, and Larry E. Westphal. "Technological Effort In Industrial Development—An Interpretative Survey Of Recent Research," *The Economics Of New Technology In Developing Countries*, 1982, pp. 105-137.

Feder, Gershon, and Roger Slade. "The Impact Of Agricultural Extension: The Training And Visit System In India," *The World Bank Research Observer*, July 1986, Vol. 1, #2, pp. 139-161.

Haavind, Robert. "Hong Kong: The Chinese Connection," *High Technology*, Nov. 1986, Vol. 6, #11, pp. 28-31.

Halberstam, David. "An Awakening Nation," *Parade*, Nov. 2, 1986, pp. 4-7.

Hann, Peter. "Galloping To Catch Up With The Japanese," *International Management*, August 1984, pp. 28-30.

Helburn, I.B. and John C. Shearer. "Human Resources And Industrial Relations In China: A Time Of Ferment," *Industrial And Labor Relations Review*, Oct. 1984, Vol. 38, #1, pp. 3-15.

Huang, Cliff J. and Faqir S. Bagi. "Technical Efficiency On Individual Farms In Northwest India," *Southern Economic Journal*, Vol. 51, #1, pp. 108-115.

Kelley, Dennis B. "A Project Manager's Notebook," *China Business Review*, Sept./Oct. 1984, Vol. 11, #5, pp. 10-12.

Khandwalla, Pradip N. "Turnaround Management Of Mismanaged Complex Organizations," *International Studies Of Management And Organization*, Winter 1983-1984, Vol. 13, #4, pp. 5-41.

Kincaid, Russell. "Korea's Major Adjustment Effort," *Finance & Development*, December 1983, Vol. 20, #4, pp. 20-23.

Marth, Del. "Lessons of Leadership: Keeping All The Lines Open," *Nation's Business*, Oct. 1984, Vol. 72, #10, pp. 85-86.

Moser, A.J. *Foreign Trade; Investment And The Law In The People's Republic Of China*, New York, Oxford University Press, 1984.

Rafferty, Kevin. "Tooling Up For The Next Surge," *Institutional Investor*, July 1983, pp. 287-290.

Roberts, Don. "Inside Story," *Training And Development Journal*, Oct. 1984, pp. 26-27.

Saner-Yui, Lichia and Raymond Saner-Yui. "Confucius Say Social Harmony More Important Than Performance," *Training And Development Journal*, Oct. 1984, pp. 28-29.

Sinha, Jai B.P. "A Model Of Effective Leadership Styles In India," *International Studies Of Management And Organization*, Summer/Fall 1984, Vol. 14, #2-3, pp. 86-98.

Westphal, Larry E. "Fostering Technological Mastery By Means Of Selective Infant-Industry Protection," *Trade, Stability, And Equity In Latin America*, 1982, pp. 255-279.

Westphal, Larry E., Linsu Kim, and Carl J. Dahlman. *Reflections On Korea's Acquisition Of Technological Capability*, Discussion Paper, Report No. DRD77, Development Research Department, Economics and Research Staff, World Bank, April 1984.

Westphal, Larry E., Yung W. Rhee, Linsu Kim, and Alice Amsden. *Exports Of Capital Goods And Related Services from the Republic Of Korea*, World Bank Staff Working Papers, No. 629, January 1984.

9

Eastern Bloc

The Eastern Bloc countries offer a study of two types of industrial culture—centrally managed economies and worker-managed factories.

One of the difficulties in looking at these countries is that there are so many of them that they could easily make up a book all by themselves. Many of their management styles are of interest to a student of management. However, it was necessary to select only those that showed benefit for Western culture and economy.

After World War II, the majority of the socialist states in Eastern Europe and Asia adopted the system of centralized planning. This was being practiced by the Soviet Union with varying degrees of success. It wasn't long before the need for increased economic efficiency was felt. Since the 1950s, attempts have been made to reform this structure, and these changes are continuing today.

The amount, extent, and timing of the reforms has varied from country to country. Some of the reform measures are efficiency-oriented, some politically motivated, and some are done out of desperation. There are, however, still some threads of commonality stemming from the ideals of these countries. As we shall see, the different reforms affected the countries in many different ways and with varying results.

In general, socialist enterprises have a threefold structure which contains these interrelated organizations—management, the party, and the trade union. Each has a separate division of duties, yet each shares certain basic processes. This is done in order to maintain a balance of the various interests involved. When we examine the management styles, we will need to observe how these three interrelate.

Economic and social pressures have complicated the rigidity of this system, and have forced it to make changes or even to break down at times. Some of the agents for this change include:

- Variety of products has greatly increased
- Rapid technological progress has taken place
- Needs of the employees have changed
- Needs of employees are widely differentiated
- People are better educated

Many reforms have occurred in the structure of the trade union organizations and in the industrial framework of participation.

A common thread of change seems to exist in all socialist bloc countries. They are all reducing the role of centralized planning and giving more autonomy to individual enterprises; there is more reliance on pricing systems to guide enterprise decision-making; and incentive systems that link the wages of managers and workers to the earnings of the enterprise are becoming common. Managers are being given more control, and the incentives help to improve their performance. The worker incentive systems help to improve productivity and to reduce the waste of resources.

Eastern European economies have become very complex, being plagued with inflation, trade deficits resulting from rising energy costs, and slow economic growth. This is causing a major crisis in the management of centrally planned economies which have become complex, moving away from economies previously dominated by agriculture. The inflexibility of the centrally planned economies has forced a breakdown of the traditional central planning methodology. Now, decentralized economic management is occurring in varying degrees in all Eastern European countries.

One of the measures taken by many of these countries is the increase in trade with the Western countries in some form of quasi-barter or in direct equity-investments. The hope is that Western technology will speed up the growth process. This forces Eastern Europe's political leaders and the communistic bureaucracies to cope with capitalism and its influences.

CUBA

Cuba had a program called Moral Economy. The slogan and central objective of this program was the creation of the "New Man." The methodology used ideologically-based economic policies, centralized planning and management, income redistribution, and a series of moral incentives which included medals and banners given as rewards to individuals and groups. Material rewards were avoided since they were considered as contradictions to the New Man who should not have individual materialistic drives.

Cuba's avoidance of materialistic incentives differed from the actions taken by many other socialistic countries. This is highlighted in this book to draw emphasis to nonmaterialistic motivators. In Cuba, we found them in existence on a nationwide basis, including a substantial amount of governmental support and fanfare.

This system, although slightly effective, soon found itself with about a 20 percent absenteeism rate in the state-civilian work force, with some areas reporting as much as 53 percent absenteeism. Productivity also experienced similar declines.

The blame for the poor results of the Moral Economy are based on:

1. Ideological property ownership policies
2. Lack of organizational forms and planning
3. Lack of motivating incentives
4. Poor personnel management

Castro blamed the failure on the fact that the populace had been too ingrained with the concepts of retaliation, the law of survival of the fittest, egotism, deceit, and exploitation. The people, he claimed, could not change their way of thinking quickly enough to implement the idealism of the Moral Economy.

Production failures and pressure from the Soviet Union to become productive forced a change in Cuba in the 1970s. It was decided that political and non-materialistic moral incentives were not enough to motivate the workers. Thereupon, economic planning and control were decentralized, price and tax systems were installed, and material incentives were introduced.

The new program involved, as Castro put it in 1971, "the merits of the workers and not just their need . . . merit is the most important factor. Societies must do the most for those who do the most for society . . . Prices will constitute a crucial factor in planning." The new policy was justified by developing the concept that first the national material base (economic strength of the nation) had to be established before socialism could be successful.

Plant profitability became the measure of performance. Some fraction of these profits was retained within the organization as an economic incentive for the organization.

Productivity improved as managers were allowed to manage their own organizations. Materialistic incentives were distributed by the tens of thousands in the form of refrigerators, radios, television sets, and pressure cookers. Cuba's productive economy was heading toward recovery.

In summary, Cuba offers us an interesting lesson in managerial philosophy and the use of incentives for motivation.

CZECHOSLOVAKIA

When we think of Eastern Bloc countries, we traditionally think of industries that are labor intensive, backward, and inefficient. We think of them as being of little interest to Westerners. However, in Czechoslovakia we find a notable exception to this misconception.

A flexible manufacturing system (FMS) is a manufacturing technique wherein a factory and its production machines are highly automated. The machines perform automatic tool selection, maintenance, and inventory control. They acquire tools from a centralized inventory location and keep track of which machine is using which tool. The first complete and most automated FMS in the world was implemented in Czechoslovakia.

In this Czechoslovakian FMS, every tool is available for all machines involved in the system. It is the most sophisticated of its type in the world. This system, funded by the Czech government, produces machine castings. It is located in two facilities: The first runs two machine centers and is close to Prague, and the second is in Olomuc and controls eight machine centers. Westerners are taking a close look at this system, and companies like Messerschmitt Bolkow-Blohm are developing systems of their own in an attempt to have comparable totally automated FMS operations.

On the negative side, Czechoslovakia is plagued with exceptionally low productivity. The Czech government is taking measures to improve the quality and efficiency of production and is gradually introducing programs that are intended to improve the attitudes of managers and workers. A secondary goal is to economize the basic production factors including raw materials usage, energy consumption, and investment efficiency. The measures being taken to realize these goals include:

1. A reinforcement of central planning.
2. The five-year plan will become the binding instrument of economic management.
3. The integration of industries into international trade organizations.
4. An increase in the number of goods subject to central planning.
5. Penalties for missing delivery times.
6. A system of economic accountability, making enterprises earn their own way. Failure to achieve goals will result in penalties that deprive producers of investment funds.
7. Prices of raw materials will be more realistic.
8. A 20 percent wage bonus if all goals are met.

The economy is moving toward an intensive effort in selected development; previous broadly defined development goals are being reduced. Investment will now be done with key objectives in mind, with an emphasis on fuels (coal and nuclear), housing, consumer goods, and automobile and truck production. In the future, the Czechoslovaks are planning to develop their electronics capability in the area of microprocessors. The development of nuclear energy and reinforced plastics is also high on their priority list. American managers can learn from the hi-tech automation in Czechoslovakian factories and should keep an eye on Czechoslovakia's technological growth. This country has the potential of becoming a major manufacturing force.

POLAND

Poland is an example of the failure of workers' councils. In the 1970s, the work force concentrated its efforts on establishing free labor unions that would give them fair representation and would look out for their interests. Solidarity emerged as the free union that became a major force, and the borders to Poland were quickly closed so that the other socialistic countries would not get "Solidarity" fever.

As with so many of the previous attempts at labor reform in the Eastern Bloc, the military was soon brought in to end the strike. However, Solidarity had matured to an advanced stage and now superseded the state-established and state-sponsored trade unions. Solidarity was an interenterprise organization and held great power. It wielded the threat of crippling the entire Polish economy.

When it felt strongest, it emerged and placed demands on the Polish state. Solidarity wanted free unions that weren't inhibited by the party doctrine. It wanted the right to strike and a guarantee of safety during a strike, and asked for a restoration of jobs and full freedom of publicity for Solidarity. It wanted freedom of speech, which was guaranteed by the Polish constitution. It asked for the appointment of managers based on their level of competence and the removal of the privilege system for members of the "party."

Solidarity proposed a "new plan" for Poland which included civil liberties, self-managed enterprises, and an improvement in economic conditions. It recommended the creation of separate enterprises, which included:

- Social—the fully independent, self-managed business that is self-financing and which implies no governmental control
- State
- Cooperative—groups of individuals working together
- Private
- Mixed

Solidarity's existence highlighted a list of problems which can be seen in the recommended solutions. The suppression of Solidarity did not remove these problems, it only hid their visibility. Today, Solidarity has been granted its legal existence as well as its place in the government of Poland. It now must try to implement its new programs successfully. Monitoring this progress should prove extremely interesting.

Before Solidarity, Poland had started programs that attempted to shift priorities and tighten controls. This was caused by the imbalance of trade and an attempt to improve the balance-of-payments deficit. Imports were being reduced and new projects would have to prove themselves as covering 120 percent of costs. This tightened economy fostered some of the additional unrest that triggered Solidarity and a new wave of reforms.

Poland, as was the case in Hungary, is one of the more assertive of the Eastern Bloc nations in searching for opportunities for economic reform within a socialistic structure. Solidarity's growth indicates this departure from many former rigidities. For example, Poland allows Western nations to set up businesses in their country which are wholly owned by the West. The management and organizational style can be completely Westernized. This is a radical departure from the "Eastern" way of doing things.

Western techniques have appeared in other ways as well, as in Poland's ongoing research with MBO (management by objectives). Many enterprises have already adapted some form of the MBO planning structure and others are planning to.

Poland serves as a good example for discussing the way the Eastern Bloc manages projects. In general, there are two types of favored projects in socialistic countries—small projects and important projects. The first is one that has received the appropriate approvals, but in general receives little support. The organization receiving the approval must come up with the resources necessary to make the project a success.

However, an important project is accorded national priority. About 150 projects of this kind exist. These are run by organizations that are allowed to override the basic governmental structure. They receive special treatment. Any organization asked to cooperate in such a project is mandated to do so, it cannot refuse and has to respond quickly, receiving strong penalties if it fails to "deliver the goods" on time. All resources, including financial and scarce resources, are readily available for a project of this type.

Approval of the project requires the acceptance of several ministries. In Poland, approval requires the consent of:

- The Party's Central Committee
- The Council of Ministers
- The Planning Commission
- The Development Commission

Unfortunately, many of the same individuals sit on several of these panels. This means that what at first appears to be a system of checks and balances is in reality nothing more than one bureaucratic approval process. Additionally, this opens the door to a considerable amount of political manipulation.

Eastern Bloc project scheduling and project progress is filled with rigidities. Contractors are not assigned to projects because they are the best for the job; rather, they are assigned because they have the political clout or because it's their turn to get a project. If the contractor performs poorly on a job, as they often do, the planning ministries and the end users try to help the contractor perform better, and the bonus system is commonly used as an incentive to encourage better performance. Consultants are brought in to attempt to improve the situation. A contractor is never fired, and when a project is completed, he is paid in full, no matter how late or how poorly he performed. The reasoning is that the weak enterprise will never be able to improve if it is not paid adequately. Additionally, with the many committees involved in every project, it becomes difficult to determine who is responsible for a failure.

Technology is also very rigid. Construction is done on a large scale. For instance, a standard set of large building panels are constructed and set up using cranes. If a project comes along that deviates from the standard set of panels, the project is changed. Projects are oriented toward the construction technology that exists, and contractors do not conform to users' needs.

Of all the "important projects" in Poland, housing is one of the top four. At first, the state tried to take over the construction of housing, but it soon realized that this could not keep up with the demand that existed. This encouraged the revival of the cooperative movement that had existed in pre-war Poland. Under this program, cooperatives are set up which include individuals who need homes. These individuals then work together to get their housing complex built. Under this program, the growth in housing was remarkable: Over 50 percent of the housing stock of Poland was constructed under this cooperative arrangement.

There are more than 1,000 cooperatives in Poland. Three types exist:

1. Tenant—the building is owned by the cooperative and the tenant has strong rights to its use.
2. Owner—the owner has full control of his apartment and can sell it.
3. Building society—a cooperative that builds housing for others. These structures are then administered on a self-governing basis by those living in the structure and the costs are shared by the users.

Originally, the state favored the tenant's cooperative but soon found that the maintenance of the housing was better under the owner's cooperative. Often, however, the costs of this form of cooperative were difficult for the limited financial resources of the future occupant. The tenant's cooperative required a 20 percent down payment and the owner's cooperative required 50 percent.

Polish citizens favored cooperative housing over state-built housing because it tended to be larger and more comfortable. The cooperatives see themselves as oriented toward satisfying the users.

Poland is continually evolving and changing. Many of these changes take the form of liberalization. Interesting information about these changes is slowly coming out of Poland, such as the articles by Gierszewska, Doktór, and Chróścicki cited at the end of this chapter. These indicate a lessening of the centralized influence and a strengthening of industrial autonomy.

Poland offers strong lessons in employee relations for both Eastern and Western managers. Solidarity demonstrated the need for the nation to get back to the basics in dealing with the workers. The success of the private housing cooperatives demonstrates how government programs can be driven to excess and that individuals don't necessarily want handouts whether they come from the government or from business enterprises. American managers need to learn when their influence is wanted and when it becomes too domineering and is therefore resented.

SOVIET UNION

The central planning model of the Soviet Union has produced significant achievements. It has helped to bring backward nations into the world of industrialization. It has supported the strong buildup of military power. It has supported price stability, full employment, and the advancement of technological development and the sciences. It has supported impressive advances in the standards of education, health, and social and private consumption.

Unfortunately, the central planning system is often criticized for being out of touch with the wishes of the general populace because its pursuits are often oriented towards the goals of its leaders.

The Soviet Union sells itself as the model for effective socialistic planning systems. Unfortunately, labor motivation is the long-standing major problem in the Soviet Union. In manufacturing, for example, there is high absenteeism and excessive idleness. Salaries are only about $400 per month in the area of manufacturing, and this is reflected in the lack of productivity.

In the past, the traditional approach of keeping total output at desired levels was to hire more workers; the additional employees made up for the lack of productivity. It also gave the Soviet Union the right to claim that it was a nation without unemployment. Eventually the point arrived where output was not up to expectations and there were no more employees available for hire. This forced the Soviet Union to embark on a productivity improvement program.

In the 1960s the Soviets started a program of developing creative job opportunities. They wanted to improve the "richness of content of work" and thereby improve worker attitudes. Unfortunately, it was eventually concluded that a disproportion existed between higher educational levels and the number of satisfying jobs.

In an attempt to improve worker motivation and to prevent union problems, Moscow is adopting the Western concept of group incentive pay and worker participation systems. Changes on the Soviet labor scene took the form of a labor reform law that took effect in August of 1983. It was passed at the same time and by the same Supreme Soviet session in which Yuri V. Andropov was elected President. Andropov was the originator of a movement for higher productivity in the Soviet labor force.

The new system allows collectives (often called brigades) of about 10 to 50 workers to have a say in planning and management. Factory managers need to have the approval of these brigades before plans can be sent to Moscow for acceptance. More importantly, brigades can determine their own staffing levels and are allowed to determine the distribution of bonuses amongst their members. Bonuses and wages are allocated based on the output of the brigade rather than by piecework.

The brigades were also given a power that had traditionally been unheard-of. They were allowed to discipline or even fire nonperformers and were held financially responsible for a lack of performance resulting in late jobs or defective parts. Productivity and wages have increased due to this plan in contrast to the traditional system of piecework wage bonuses.

Strikes are still not allowed. However, the drafting of the 1983 labor reform law occurred just after Solidarity emerged in Poland. Soviet leaders became conscious of the threat of strikes and began to make plans that they hoped would prevent the occurrence of strikes in their country. Still, Soviet workers recognize that many of their East European partners enjoy a higher standard of living and freer labor organizations. Soviet leaders realize this and are starting to give their own workers more freedom, but it will be a long time before they go as far as the worker councils of Poland and Yugoslavia.

The Soviet government needs to decide whether to maintain this nontraditional approach. The existing Soviet bureaucracy is resistive to these dramatic changes, but the current leadership still sees them as being necessary.

Shifts from agriculture toward a consumer product industry will require the Soviets to reduce the enormous labor force now working in agriculture. The United States, with only four percent of its labor force employed in agriculture, far outproduces the Soviets with 20 percent employed in this area. Efficiency and technological advances are the first steps that are planned to make this shift, but realizing the need for this shift does not assure that it will happen.

Although it is generally felt that improvements in the Soviet Union must begin in agriculture, little appears to be changing in this sector. The migration of more automated production methods is also extremely slow; there is a shortage of skilled mechanics and machine operators; the average age of the farm worker is growing older, and no incentive programs have been installed that might help to increase output. All these factors combined seem to indicate a decrease in productive output on the government-run farms in the future.

If efficiency is to be improved, it must begin at the management level. For example, the management of the large government-run farms is so inefficient that the small, private, family-run garden plots are believed to produce as much as 10 times the output of the government farms.

The performance measurement systems of the Soviet Union foster a resistance to change. Managers are assigned to produce a certain output, and the closer this output is to what they had to produce last year, the easier it is to meet the goal. Any change in output opens the door for failure. This measurement system exists throughout the central planning system. The result is that no one in the system wants change, especially changes as dramatic as those initiated by Andropov.

The Soviet government is trying to change this resistance, first by changing the performance measurements, and second by establishing an enormous training program for managers. The new program takes two years and involves mostly full-time study. One month is spent working at the State Planning Committee and another working at the appropriate ministry office under which the manager will work. At the end of the program, the students must write a thesis and present an oral defense.

The Soviets dwell on the idea that every problem has an "optimal" solution and, given enough time to research the problem, the optimum can be found. This is incorporated into their management training. Operations research techniques are a major portion of the training programs for managers wherein they are taught to always search for optimal solutions.

In general, the Soviet approach to management is a systems approach that involves the application of scientific methods. The training program of a manager starts with a study of Marxist-Leninist economic theory. It covers the theory and practice of management, the scientific organization of labor, economic incentives, economic-mathematical modeling, and computer technology. The method of training includes lectures and seminars but emphasizes case studies and business games in an attempt to simulate real management processes.

One successful employee motivator that the Soviets have used involves a group of "inventors or innovators" who receive special recognition for introducing creative ways in which to make their operation run more efficiently. They also receive trips to other plants in the Soviet Union where they inspect different plant operations. The hope is that they will bring home ideas that can be used in their own plants. The Soviet Union boasts several million dollars worth in cost reductions as a result of this program. The employee's reward is to receive published recognition and a free trip.

A more detailed study of Soviet management styles are the excellent articles by Boris Milner cited at the end of this chapter. Mr. Milner is a lecturer at the National Institute of Economic Management in Moscow and heads a management team that studies management problems in the Soviet Union.

The rigid structure of the Soviet government might create expectations that problems can be solved quickly and easily. Unfortunately, the rigidity of the bureaucracy and the problem of negotiating with committees causes progress to be very slow. The result is that the Soviet people are tired of governmental rhetoric. They are pushing for results that will benefit them *now*. Recently, on a local call-in talk show where a governmental planning official was hosted, a housewife was quoted as saying; "I've had enough of your five-year plans and phony promises, I want to know what you (the government authorities) are doing for me now!" There was no response from the official.

TURKEY

Some people might argue with the notion of classifying Turkey as an Eastern Bloc country. However, because of its large number of state-owned enterprises, this is the chapter where Turkey best fits.

After World War I, when Turkey was a young nation, its leaders pushed for rapid growth and development. The lack of trained managers, entrepreneurs, and engineers encouraged them to look at both Soviet and Western models for industrial development. The decision was made that developmental efforts should be regionalized and channeled in two directions—the private enterprise and the state-controlled enterprise.

In theory, although not in practice, state enterprises function the same way as efficient private enterprises. Theoretically, the state enterprises are to function in those areas where the state can do better. As private enterprises become viable in those areas, the state enterprises are to be "sold out" in shares until they are no longer under state control.

What has happened is that the state enterprise has become responsible not just for the industry but also the infrastructure. The state enterprise has become responsible for ports, housing, schools, roads, health and recreational facilities, and so on. Even job security is assured. This prevents the burdened state enterprise from becoming a competitive entity when private enterprises compete with it.

Those areas where private enterprises are large enough to take hold receive state support. The ideal is that the state and private enterprises find their own levels of efficiency, but when the private sector becomes large enough to compete with the state sector, conflicts in product competitiveness arise.

In Turkey, the state has a firm stronghold in enterprises such as steel, mining, fertilizers, petrochemicals, pulp, and paper. There appears to be little possibility in the near future that any form of private enterprise will be taking control of these capital-intensive industries.

Turkey has developed an interesting model for observation. It has avoided the Soviet model where the individual is suppressed while at the same time avoiding the capitalistic model. The state has taken the role as leader in planning and development and prevents any private organization from taking a dominating role at the expense of anyone else in the social structure.

However, as in all models, there are some failures. In the case of the Turkish state manufacturing complex, a self-perpetuating power group has been developed that links bureaucrats, labor unions, and local politicians. The control that this group fosters is deemed more powerful than that of any private-power blocs that can be established. Additionally, the dualism that occurs in many areas has developed a strong antagonism between state and private enterprises; they are not mutually supportive. Also, the state-run enterprises are far from being efficient and well-managed, which makes them poor role models for private enterprises to follow.

Turkey has shown impressive growth in manufacturing output. The manufacturing industry is considered the primary tool for rapid growth and self-sufficiency. The main instrument that encourages industrial growth is a generous industrial incentive system which includes tax breaks, interest subsidies, export tax rebates, duty-free imports, appropriately placed tariffs and import quotas, and the retention of export earnings. Resources are channeled to public sector investments that support basic industries geared to produce export products.

With its population of about 43 million, Turkey has an enormous appetite for Western goods, and Westerners are trying their utmost to sell them as much as possible. However, with the industrial incentives that have been established, most of this market is being recaptured internally. In addition, exceptionally high tariff rates have been placed on finished goods imports, and resources for manufacturing processes are brought into the country duty-free.

Turkey still lacks the ability to step into a truly competitive environment that forces efficiency. Due to the national system of protectionism, most firms find they do not need to deal with competition. The demand for products is great, generally greater than supply, allowing the producing firms to set whatever prices they deem appropriate. This allows them to cover any excessive costs. However, although the firms employ inefficient, high-cost production methods, the long-term hope is that they will push for efficiency and become competitive in the international marketplace. To do this, they have been given the proper incentives, such as export interest and tax allowances. A detailed evaluation of the effectiveness of the incentive systems, explaining how and when adjustments had to be made, is given in the report by Yagci cited at the end of this chapter.

Along with inefficient production methods, another cost of the high productive increases found in Turkey is the deterioration of income distribution for the citizens. The industrial segment has experienced a productivity increase of about four to five times that of the agricultural sector. This has caused a migration from the field to the factory, and the industrial sector has not been able to absorb the surplus labor.

Turkey offers us lessons about the efficiency and effectiveness of state-operated industrial complexes, and offers some lessons about state enterprises that compete with private industry. It appears that state enterprises are not effective competitors, especially in an international marketplace.

YUGOSLAVIA

In 1948, Yugoslavia was the first Soviet Bloc country to drop out of the Soviet planning mold with the expulsion of the Cominform System.[1] From this point on it moved towards the total removal of the central planning system. In 1965 it allowed self-managed enterprises to respond to market forces as they saw fit. Due to these changes, Yugoslavia has long been a country of interest to Westerners, Easterners, and developing countries. Westerners see Yugoslavia as a successful example of worker enterprise management, and many lessons can be learned from the Yugoslav experience on how such enterprises should be structured and organized.

For the Eastern European countries, Yugoslavia offers an example of decentralization. It shows how much of the central-control bureaucracy can be eliminated without sacrificing any ideals.

For developing countries that suffer from a lack of management expertise

---

[1]This is the standard of centralized planning.

or who want to reduce the disparity between the rich and the poor, Yugoslavia offers a way for the worker to control some of his own destiny. Yugoslavia is establishing new enterprises in areas of the country that are as underdeveloped as are many other developing countries. The latter can learn by observing the process that Yugoslavia uses to establish worker-run enterprises.

The self-management concept was born during the National Liberation War in 1941. At this time, Yugoslavia was centrally planned. During the 1940s and 1950s, the centralized control was gradually decentralized and a move toward a stronger self-management system was born out of a philosophy of social ownership of the production processes. A closer link between the workers and the conditions and fruits of their labors was sought.

In 1974, the management philosophy was decentralized even more, taking the form of constitutional reform. A decentralized planning process was constructed with multiple points of power. The basic economic unit became the BOAL (Basic Organization of Associated Labor), rather than the firm or enterprise.

The Yugoslavs had learned that there was a conflict between central planning and worker self-management. Centralized management left few decisions to be made at the organizational level. Yugoslavia's planners were forced to decentralize and to establish communication systems among organizations rather than feeding everything through the central planning system the way it is done in most socialistic countries.

By decentralizing, the self-management groups were able to improve the performance of their own enterprises. Incentive systems were widely established. A link was established that attached all workers' incomes to the performance of their enterprise in the marketplace. This forced involvement and participation onto the entire labor force, thus affecting all aspects of production. The result is seen in improved performance and efficiency in the enterprises.

Within an enterprise, workers meet to establish production rates and wage rates. They determine what to produce, how to produce it, how long they should work, and under what conditions they should work. They determine their own reinvestment and expansion plans and their bonuses.

Within each shop of the enterprise, separate units promote the interest of their particular groups. These units are called BOALs. United, the BOALs form the enterprise and create its policies. BOALs are organized into OALs (Organization of Associated Labor), and several OALs make up a COAL (Composite Organization of Labor). It is unclear at what level the association is considered an enterprise, since this can occur at different levels, depending on the business. However, the BOALs are the critical unit and have a great deal of independence. The worker's income comes directly from the BOAL, not from the larger enterprise, even though an economic interconnection exists between BOALs, OALs, and COALs.

Self-management of the enterprise is the responsibility of the BOALs. Joint decisions are made at this level and representatives are elected who have the authority to vote for the BOALs at the OAL level. At the enterprise level, management for the enterprise is hired by the BOAL representatives, and this team is responsible to them. It is management's responsibility to carry out the plans established by the BOALs.

Whenever different groups of individuals with different sets of goals are working together, conflicts arise. In Yugoslavia, these conflicts far too often result in wildcat strikes, and it becomes the responsibility of the workers' councils to resolve these conflicts by coming up with compromise solutions. Strikes are seldom reported in the media because they may create sympathetic reactions in other parts of the country. However, it is estimated that, on the average, there is one isolated strike in Yugoslavia every two days. These are often dealt with by dismissal of the strike leaders, trade union leaders, or party leaders, and by fines. In general, strikes are not considered "appropriate"; the BOALs and workers' councils are considered the only acceptable avenues for resolving conflicts.

Within the BOALs, elected representatives are restricted to no more than one term in office at a time. The representative may be reelected later after someone else has had a turn as representative. The BOAL meetings are held monthly, and it is at these meetings that nearly all decisions affecting the BOAL are made.

There is a tremendous amount of social and political pressure exerted on the self-management system in order to keep it in line. For example, managers who attempt to dominate the decision-making process are labeled "class enemies." Workers who take advantage of the system but are uninterested in it by being apathetic about the voting or decision-making process are labeled "little citizens."

In studying Yugoslavia and its unique management style, we find an example of a country that doesn't fit the mold of many other socialistic countries. As an example, Yugoslavia's project management techniques don't fit the descriptions that I have outlined in the section on Poland for the typical project. Yugoslavia enjoys a greater degree of decentralization, enterprise autonomy, and self-management.

Yugoslavian enterprises have a great deal of freedom in the selection of projects and the appointment of project management. Guidelines are set and certain projects receive governmental favor in funding, but overall, the enterprise is free to decide whether the project is worthwhile or not. Enterprise performance is more important than in other Eastern Bloc countries, and the use of project management techniques is more prevalent.

Yugoslavia's strong compensation system is based on cost controls. The incomes of the enterprise and its workers are directly affected by cost overruns and poor financial and managerial controls. Profit-sharing is a major part of the pay in almost every project, with the employees receiving only a minimal wage initially with the understanding that they will receive a share of the profits later (as much as two-thirds of their initial wage).

The Works Council of the Yugoslavian government is highly involved in the selection of projects and is also involved in determining which employees are assigned to which project. Once selected, the management of the project requires tight control. This often causes the self-management concept to be dropped and a democratic control system to be forfeited. A more militaristic approach is required and used. Decisions must be reached quickly, and one individual is placed in charge and given the responsibility for these decisions. At the conclusion of the project, a report is submitted to the Works Council for final approval. This organization then divides the profits.

Like so many of the Eastern Bloc countries, Yugoslavia has major problems in regional development. Some areas of the country are very advanced while others are sadly backwards. One might speculate that, with the centralized planning structure found in many countries, it should be easy to allocate resources to those areas that are in need. Unfortunately, the central planning process has strong political overtones; individuals in influential positions often use their power for political gains. There is a lack of consistency between goals and the policies that would reduce regional differences. In the case of Yugoslavia, the general consensus is that it needs a firm political commitment to solve this problem before anything more can be accomplished.

Yugoslavia allows more freedom of travel than other Eastern Bloc countries. This has given it a work force of better-trained individuals, but at the price of higher wage expectations. "Guest workers" who return from Europe are voting for high, Western-type salary increases, thus causing their products to be less price-competitive.

The self-management concept also has its drawbacks. Endless worker meetings often tend to drain the energies of both workers and management, and the intricate levels of BOALs, OALs, and COALs make the decision-making process slow and cumbersome. Additionally, the strong Western influence that was allowed by Tito has made Yugoslavia a nation of mixed ideals which blends both Eastern and Western philosophy into a type of market socialism.

Nevertheless, Yugoslavia offers United States managers one of the most interesting examples of worker-enterprise management in the world. The use of BOALs and workers' councils has established a successful form of worker-enterprise autonomy. This country also offers a valuable lesson in the failure of centralized management, a lesson that many American corporations have not yet learned.

SOME OTHER COUNTRIES

Bulgaria

Bulgaria tries to conform to Moscow's orthodox communistic doctrine and is more hesitant than most Eastern Bloc countries to relax central controls. It is moving towards economic reforms, though not as substantial as the reforms that have occurred in Hungary.

East Germany

East Germany is one of the more conservative of the Eastern European nations. It strives to maintain the orthodox communistic doctrine of Moscow. However, it is feeling the pressures of a very complex society and is introducing economic reforms.

Hungary

In Hungary, we find the replacement of the traditional trade union councils which are no longer the central institutions of democracy. The trade union committees now only serve as executive organs and are no longer a major influence in enterprise decisions. Now, the shop stewards' committees are the highest institution of workers' participation and are also the highest trade union organization in an enterprise. In this manner, the interests of various groups of employees are defended more effectively, and the enormous bureaucracy that the trade unions imposed on enterprises has been reduced.

Hungary's philosophy of autonomy for enterprises has removed some of the central control of projects that is felt by many countries. For example, an enterprise is now free to make a contract with another enterprise without the direct approval of the central ministries that oversee it.

Hungary is shifting to a reliance on its market to determine costs and to set prices. The market guides investment decisions, allocates labor and other resources, and makes industry more competitive internationally. Plant-wide lay-offs have occurred, which have been unheard-of in the past. The worker no longer has the unqualified right to his job. If the industry is not profitable, it gets shut down!

Hungary is venturing into new forms of technology. For example, their research in holography is unique and advanced. United States producers of laser products have found a good market in this technological development, and they find that Eastern Europeans are willing to pay cash for advanced equipment and technology.

Romania

In Romania, the state central planning agency determined the specifications for major product lines and sets overall production goals. However, organizations that perform well are receiving some autonomy. For example, Romania's 23 August Works facilities are now using management reporting tools, such as sales reports, that were previously unheard-of since marketing was under the control of a separate agency. Before this, little was known about how the products were selling and about customer acceptance of the products.

With these changes, August Works now has a better picture of its export performance and so can modify its product mix to some extent in order to maximize export sales. The central planning group still determines the volumes of production, but the August Works now has control over the mix of products that are produced.

Within the organization, the members of the nine-man management team are elected annually by the workers, but this is nothing more than a formality without any real campaigning. Workers also elect a 27-member working peoples' committee which must approve all management decisions and disciplinary actions. There are also a union representative and two communist party representatives on the decision-making team.

While keeping with the ideological rhetoric, Romania has moved more and more with an eye towards the West. Unlike most East European countries, Romania's trade with the West and with developing countries has now exceeded that of trade within Comecom (Council for Mutual Economic Assistance), the inter-Eastern European trading association.

SUMMARY

The Eastern Bloc offers many lessons for Westerners about managing employees, businesses and managers, and about the effects of incentive programs. It has the appearance of being an ideal place to try different methodologies under a controlled environment. Unfortunately, though, many times this environment is not as controlled as we might believe.

The flow of information is restricted in socialistic countries. As an example, a national computer network was planned for installation in one of these countries. This seemed like an ideal environment since everything was controlled from the top down in an integrated manner. This indicated that data should be collected from the bottom up. The additional control advantage that this would offer would be enormous. This project carried with it the promise of a more prosperous economy, and received national approval as an "important project."[2]

As implementation began, many of the ministers who had previously approved the project now began to realize that they were offering their superiors—as well as other organizations—information that would allow these groups to monitor their progress. There was a sudden clampdown on information; the ministers became afraid that the balance of power would be shifted away from them, and they did not want to be controlled. The ministers at the very top of the political structure declined to support the project any further. Therefore, because of the lack of available data and cooperation, the project soon failed.

This possessiveness of data and the fear that the additional freedom of information will allow an organization to be controlled by superiors or other organizations can also be found in Western bureaucracies; it is not unique to the

---

[2]Read the section on Poland for the explanation of an "important project."

East. However, with the central planning structure of the East, one might have hoped that it could resolve this problem and thus benefit greatly.

The Eastern Bloc countries are desperately trying to develop and improve the living standards of their people, and are promoting advances in efficiency in an attempt to achieve this goal. To this end, they are moving at varying speeds. For example, Poland's debt-service ratio has been around 50%, the highest of all, while Czechoslovakia has been the most conservative and has attempted to avoid financing its growth with debt.

In pushing for growth, countries such as East Germany and Bulgaria have looked to Moscow for aid, while others such as Romania and Poland are taking lessons from the West. In many countries, operations are now co-owned by both Eastern and Western partners. In the case of Poland, businesses are wholly owned by Westerners. Clark Equipment Company, Corning Glass Works, Levi Strauss, Control Data, International Harvester, and General Motors are examples of the many companies that now have plants in the Eastern Bloc.

The United States is not the only benefactor in this East-West relationship. For example, Bulgaria is jointly operating a gambling casino in Sofia with a Lebanese firm, and the casino sits in a hotel financed by a Japanese firm.

As the Eastern Bloc moves more and more towards capitalistic business styles, Western countries will receive new opportunities for trade and investment. Many bloc countries are willing to pay cash for advanced engineering and high-technology products, but a shift is forming away from cash payments towards "compensation" packages which tie sales to purchases of their own products. A good place to start in an analysis of East-West trade relationships, and how these relationships should be established, can be found in the article by Hayden cited at the end of this chapter.

In this push for change, most of the Soviet countries—excluding Turkey and Yugoslavia—have maintained their principle of central planning. Even Czechoslovakia, the most radical in its blueprint for reform, is maintaining this policy. For most of these countries, regulated-market mechanisms have assisted in making changes more efficient, and the majority—including the Soviet Union—have announced some form of decentralization of the decision-making process that facilitates the use of these mechanisms.

REFERENCES

Anonymous. "Capitalistic Troubles For Eastern Europe," *Business Week*, August 13, 1979, pp. 40,41,44,48.

Anonymous. "Czechoslovakia—Planners Scale Down Objectives Originally Intended For 1980; Consider Orientation Of Economy For The Next Five Years," *Business America*, November 17, 1980, Vol. 3, #23, pp. 26-28.

Anonymous. "Moscow Tries To Light A Fire Under Its Workers," *Business Week*, August 1, 1983, p. 44.

Anonymous. "Participative Decision Making: A Comparative Study," *Industrial Relations*, Fall 1979, Vol. 18, #3, pp. 295-309.

Anonymous. "Poland—Government Takes Firm Control Of Investment Outlays; Many Opportunities Exist For Industrial Cooperation," *Business America*, Sept. 10, 1979, Vol. 2, #19, pp. 20-21.

Anonymous. "Turkey—Credit Is Key To Selling This Market Of 43 Million; Loans To Finance Imports Are Actively Sought," *Business America*, Sept. 10, 1979, Vol. 2, #19, p. 23.

Bertsch, Gary K. "Participation And Influence In Yugoslav Self-Management," *Industrial Relations*, Fall 1979, Vol. 18, #3, pp. 322-329.

Brand, Horst. "Solidarity's Proposals For Reforming Poland's Economy," *Monthly Labor Review*, May 1982, Vol. 105, #5, pp. 43-46.

Carlson, Elliot. "Rumanian Factory Gets More Managerial Scope," *International Management*, Aug, 1974, Vol. 29, #8, pp. 35-37.

Chandler, Margaret K. "Project Management In The Socialist Bloc," *Columbia Journal Of World Business*, Summer 1978, Vol. 13, #2, pp. 71-86.

Chróscicki, Zbigniew. "Management By Objectives In A Socialist Enterprise," *International Studies Of Management and Organization*, Fall 1980, Vol. 10, #3, pp. 91-101.

Clutterbuck, David. "Soviet Union Taps Shop Floor Talents," *International Management*, May 1978, Vol. 33, #5, pp. 53-54.

Constable, John. "Managing The USSR," *Management Today*, Sept. 1984, pp. 78-82.

Dahlman, Carl J., Bruce Ross-Larson, and Larry E. Westphal. *Managing Technological Development—Lessons From Newly Industrializing Countries*, World Bank Staff Working Papers, No. 717, January 1985.

Doktór, Kazimierz. "Changes In The System Of Managing Industry In A Socialist Economy," *International Studies Of Management And Organization*, Fall 1980, Vol. 10, #3, pp. 7-26.

Estrin, Saul and Michael Connock. "Ideas Of Industrial Democracy In Eastern Europe: A Comment From The Yugoslav Perspective," *ACES Bulletin*, Spring 1983, Vol. 25, #1, pp. 67-74.

Gierszewska, Grazyna. "Higher-Level Authorities' Influence On Decision Making In Business Organizations," *International Studies Of Management And Organization*, Fall 1980, Vol. 10, #3, pp. 57-69.

Gutsenko, K. and B. Zharkov. "Judicial Protection Of Labour Rights In The USSR," *International Labour Review*, Nov./Dec. 1982, Vol. 121, #6, pp. 731-745.

Hayden, Eric W. "Transferring Technology To The Soviet Bloc—U.S. Corporate Experience," *Research Management*, Sept. 1976, Vol. 19, #5, pp. 17-23.

Hethy, L. "Trade Unions, Shop Stewards, And Participation In Hungary," *International Labour Review*, July/August 1981, Vol. 120, #4, pp. 491-503.

Himmetoglu, Buelent A. "Personnel—Administration Practices In Turkish Industrial Firms," *International Studies Of Management And Organization*, Fall 1982, Vol. 12, #3, pp. 73-81.

Holesovsky, Vaclav. "Ideas Of Industrial Democracy In Eastern Europe: Dilemmas And Blind Alleys," *ACES Bulletin (Association For Comparative Economic Studies)*, Summer 1981, Vol. 23, #2, pp. 71-79.

Jackson, Marvin R. "Agricultural Output In Southeastern Europe, 1910-1938," *ACES Bulletin*, Winter 1982, Vol. 24, #4, pp. 49-87.

Kelly, Joe. "Participative Management: Can It Work?" *Business Horizons*, August 1980, Vol. 23, #4, pp. 74-79.

Knight, Peter T. "Social Reform: Moving Inexorably Towards Change," *Report: News And Views From The World Bank*, August-September 1983, pp. 7-8.

Kolaja, Jiri. "World-Wide Interest In Worker Participation In Management," *American Journal Of Economics And Sociology*, April 1982, Vol. 41, #2, pp. 211-213.

Markish, Yuri and Anton F. Malish. "The Soviet Food Program: Prospects For The 1980's," *ACES Bulletin*, Spring 1983, Vol. 25, #1, pp. 47-65.

Meyer, Herbert E. "Helping The Soviet Union To Avoid An Energy Crisis," *Fortune*, Jan. 29, 1979, Vol. 99, #2, pp. 90-95.

Milenkovitch, Deborah Duff. "Self Management And Thirty Years Of Yugoslav Experience," *ACES Bulletin*, Fall 1983, Vol. 25, #3, pp. 1-26.

Milner, B.Z. "A Systems Approach To The Management Of Soviet Firms," *International Studies Of Management And Organization*, Spring/Summer 1979, Vol. 9, #2, pp. 58-75.

Milner, Boris. "The Soviet View Of Management," *International Management*, March 1972, Vol. 27, #3. pp. 17-20.

Moran, Robert T. "Theory Z: But Not Japan," *S.A.M. Advanced Management Journal*, Autumn 1983, pp. 27-33.

Nishimizu, Mieko and John M. Page, Jr. "Total Factor Productivity Growth, Technological Progress, And Technical Efficiency Change—Dimensions Of Productivity Change In Yugoslavia, 1965-78," *The Economic Journal*, Dec. 1982, Vol. 92, pp. 920-936.

Oral, Muhittin, Jean-Louis Malouin, and Joel Rahn. "Formulating Technology Policy And Planning Industrial R&D Activities," *Management Science*, Nov. 1981, Vol. 27, #11, pp. 1294-1308.

Partridge, Simon. "Why Management Won't Transfer," *Management Today*, July 1980, pp. 25-26.

Phillips, James C. and Joseph E. Benson. "Some Aspects Of Job Satisfaction In The Soviet Union," *Personnel Psychology*, Autumn 1983, Vol. 36, #3, pp. 633-645.

Pleskovic, Boris and Marjan Dolenc. "Regional Development In A Socialist, Developing, And Multinational Country—The Case Of Yugoslavia," *International Regional Science Review*, May 1982, Vol. 7, #1, pp. 1-24.

Ramondt, Joop. "Workers' Self-Management And Its Constraints: The Yugoslav Experience," *British Journal Of Industrial Relations*, March 1979, Vol. 17, #1, pp. 83-94.

Roca, Sergio. "Moral Incentives In Socialist Cuba," *Association For Comparative Economic Studies Bulletin*, Summer 1980, Vol. 22, #2, pp. 33-52.

Semenov, A. "Workers' Participation In Occupational Safety And Health In The USSR," *International Labour Review*, May/June 1983, Vol. 122, #3, pp. 355-366.

Sullivan, Sherman R. "Implications Of Production Functions: Yugoslav Economic Growth—1952-1974," *American Economist*, Fall 1983, Vol. 27, #2, pp. 67-73.

Wälstedt, Bertil. *State Manufacturing Enterprise In A Mixed Economy, The Turkish Case*, Baltimore, The World Bank, The John Hopkins University Press, 1980.

Weimer, George A. "Automating Tool Selection Still Unfulfilled Promise," *Iron Age*, Nov. 25, 1983, Vol. 226, #28, pp. 98-105.

Yagci, Fahrettin. *Protection And Incentives In Turkish Manufacturing*, The World Bank, May 1984.

Zwerdling, Daniel. *Workplace Democracy: A Guide To Workplace Ownership, Participation, And Self-management Experiments In The United States And Europe*, New York, Harper Colophon Books, Harper & Row Publishers, 1980, pp. 159-166.

10

Developing Countries

Up to now, this book has demonstrated that there is not one "best" way to manage an organization or run a factory. We should realize that the United States labor-oriented method of management is in fact inappropriate in many instances. This dramatically comes to light when we investigate management problems in developing countries.

In many cases, such a country has high unemployment problems. Labor efficiency is near the bottom of the priority list. A lack of jobs is a prevalent situation, and this encourages make-work environments throughout the country.

Realizing this, why do United States managers insist on applying United States methods in plants installed in developing countries? Is it because they don't know any better? Is it because they don't understand anything but a labor-oriented management style?

Most production systems outside the U.S. do not fall into the "United States" or "Japanese" models. Most developing countries have specific problems that they must resolve, such as space restrictions, untrained work forces, or distribution restrictions. Often, simply obtaining electricity or installing a telephone system may require years.

To enable you to better understand some of the difficulties that exist in developing countries, I will review two specific examples, one in Mexico and one in Indonesia. These will highlight a few of the problems that developing countries have in their factories, such as differences in production methodologies, production objectives, logistics problems, and communications.

T IN Q, MEXICO

The city Q is the home of T and is a major industrial city north of Mexico City. T is a division of a major United States manufacturer. It employs approximately 6,000 people. T is a discrete manufacturer (both fabrication and assembly) of transmissions for automobiles, buses, and small trucks. It also has a small satellite facility a few blocks away that produces forklifts and front-end loaders.

The top levels of management at T are primarily United States citizens. The second and third levels of management are, for the most part, Mexicans trained in the United States or who are heavily indoctrinated in the U.S. way of doing things. Additionally, there always seems to be a sufficient number of U.S. "advisors" sent by either the home office or one of the U.S. automobile manufacturers. These advisors work on the factory floor and try to keep production running smoothly.

The work force on the factory floor is largely unskilled. The average employee even has difficulty in filling out time sheets. Most of the production that is scheduled is done by the "expediting" method, which means it isn't scheduled at all. Management has tried to implement educational programs and even has a staff of full-time instructors and classrooms, but the need for a more complete education of the work force far exceeds the capacity of these facilities.

An adversarial relationship has developed between the average worker and the rich Mexican boss. The average worker resents the non-Mexican who has to communicate with him through an interpreter and who makes him feel inadequate. Mexican middle management resents the feeling that North Americans think Mexicans aren't good enough to run the plant.

Production scheduling is a blend of computer-generated MRP schedules wherein production plans are changed by expeditors trying to feed assembly. This schedule is then corrected by non-Mexican advisors who try to push through their pet production jobs. This schedule is in turn overridden by top management trying to please U.S. customers.

The goals of the average factory floor worker are quite different than those of his counterpart in the United States. The worker does not see himself as a part of the company, trying to make it a success. He rarely searches for opportunities to work overtime in order to make more money; rather, he looks for an opportunity to spend as much time as possible with his family. One of the biggest problems that T experiences is that after an employee receives a paycheck, he may not show up for work for several days. Once he again feels the financial necessity to work, he returns.

The selection of foreman or shop supervisors is very difficult. There is no predefined system for evaluating an individual's potential, such as a level of education or grades in school. For the poorer citizens, there is very little opportunity to determine the jobs for which they are best-suited. As a result, promotions often occur through relatives or friends. Occasionally, bribes influence a promotion, and so not necessarily the most qualified individuals are moved up in the organization.

Strikes occur regularly in Mexico, and this forces a total shutdown of not only the production facility, but also of all business offices. This can create enormous management problems. For example, at T, both plants—transmission and forklift—do all their data processing work, including production scheduling, at the larger facility. A strike at this facility severely handicaps the second facility which may not be on strike.

The scheduling of raw material receipts is complex and sporadic. Border crossings require customs, bribes, and time delays. In order to keep production flowing, raw materials are stockpiled, even more so than in the United States.

Equipment maintenance is dependent upon scavenging; it has become easier to replace a broken part in a machine by finding the same part in a similar machine. This brings the needed machine on line quicker with less chance of a repair error. As a result of this practice, several machines throughout the facility are basically worthless except for their value as spare parts.

The number of scrapped parts due to obsolescence, operational error, or overproduction is enormous. Forged gears, several years old and red with rust, are piled high in the yards. Work-in-process inventory is unreasonably high, and the majority of the factory floor is used for inventory storage. Bins of parts that haven't been moved for months or possibly even years can be found throughout the plant.

Quality is poor because of the lack of training and the lack of any organized system to improve quality. On one occasion, the quality of producing a particular part was so bad that it was cheaper to ship the forged part to Japan, have it ground and cut, and then ship the finished part back to Mexico for assembly in a transmission. This was actually a cost saving over T's high scrap rate in spite of shipment costs and higher labor costs.

The infrastructure also presents many problems. The facility has to maintain its own power-enhancement equipment as protection against power surges and brown-outs. It can take as much as one year to install telephones and telex systems. Equipment purchases are accorded the same lengthy delays.

These are just some of the problems that are not handled by "modern" American production methodologies. Many of these problems also exist in factories in the United States, such as the problem with excessive work-in-process inventory. It is important to realize, though, that many of these problems in Mexico are very different from those of a counterpart factory in the United States, and therefore their solutions do not fit into the U.S. mold.

A detailed analysis of how to resolve many of T's problems could fill volumes. Our analysis here will be brief in order to highlight possible solutions. As always, an analysis should start with the basics. As stated earlier in this book, there are three areas of control—materials, labor, and machinery. Taking these one at a time, we can review what is happening at T and apply some techniques for improvement based on what we have stated so far.

In analyzing the labor at T, we find job standards and an efficiency reporting system that keep track of the performance of each employee. The United States philosophy of controlling each individual has been incorporated here, but is labor efficiency a goal of T?

The Mexican government gives T incentives to employ as many people as possible, and this makes it advantageous to overstaff. This brings to light the fact that the goal of the Mexican government is full employment, and two of T's goals are:

1. To keep the government happy and
2. To promote the governmental goal of full employment.

With these goals in mind, is the goal of employee efficiency, which suggests that each employee do as much work as possible, realistic? No! Factory floor automation is also inconsistent with these goals. Hiring more workers to do the jobs that automation can do is more in line with the goals of T.

Also in line with the goals of T and Mexico would be a better training program as is found in many of the countries we have studied. For example, spending as much as two months per year in education—teaching the employee reading, writing, math, and gardening, or any other subjects of interest—would give the employer a better employee. It would also give T a basis of evaluating who would make the better supervisor when future promotions are considered.

In the case of materials, T has a high raw-materials inventory, which is justified because of the excessive lead time for raw materials caused by the border crossing. As was already stated, raw materials is the cheapest of the three types of inventory (followed by work-in-process and then finished goods). If inventory must be stored, it should be stored as cheaply as possible—as raw materials.

In the area of machinery, we have already established that T should avoid automation. We also recognize the need for scavenging as a means to keep needed equipment in operable condition. Although this system seems foolish to the typical United States manager, let's consider its advantages:

1. The employee knows where to find the part without a (lengthy) catalog search.
2. The employee can see how it is supposed to look and how it should fit into the machine.
3. The equipment used is generally old and was most likely purchased second-hand from the United States. Keeping an extra machine strictly for spare parts may not be too costly.
4. Very few individuals are needed with the ability to order spare parts. These individuals would spend their time rebuilding the "spare parts" machines after pieces have been taken out. Ordering parts is much eas-

ier since you now have a machine to look at. The pressure to get the machine operational is off since it is only a spare parts machine.

Reviewing the three areas of emphasis (materials, labor, and machinery), which is the most critical to manage in the T environment? Not labor, since to have excess is advantageous and fits the goals of the company and the country. Not machinery, since having extra "spare parts" machines is also advantageous. However, inventory is costly because of high interest rates, and currently, inventory levels are out-of-hand. Several inventory-oriented management systems have been highlighted in this book, and any one of them would offer better production management than what T is now experiencing.

N IN B, INDONESIA

B is a city on the island of Java in Indonesia. This city is the home of N, a military aircraft manufacturing facility. It is a discrete manufacturer primarily involved in assembly, with plans to expand the level of vertical integration to include the fabrication of all necessary components.

The top levels of management are primarily foreign-trained, with many of them holding Ph.D. degrees from major universities in the United States. The work force is largely unskilled and uneducated, but the relationship between the employer and employee is much closer than that in the Mexican facility. The labor force is easier to manage and is more relaxed than that of T.

Problems similar to those of T are found in the source and quality of raw materials. The infrastructure problems are even worse than those of T because good roads are practically nonexistent. Those that do exist are shared by tanks as well as cars and trucks.

The market for N's products—small planes and helicopters—is entirely within Indonesia. N hopes to produce parts for foreign markets in the future, such as Boeing.

Now, an interesting conflict in technology and labor force utilization has arisen. N wants to do sophisticated design work, yet the majority of their labor force has a limited ability to read and write. The primary national goal in Indonesia, as in Mexico, is full employment, and automation would defeat this objective. Indonesia has a very limited, highly trained technical work force, but the abilities of these technicians need to be increased with advanced technology. The solution to this appears to require the introduction of high-tech disciplines such as CAD (computer-aided design) along with as *little* automation as possible in the production area.

With regard to the management of labor, materials, and machinery, many of the same conclusions can be reached as with T. However, the spread between the educational levels of the employees and management is much broader. So, an educational program for the employees must be more extensive.

A management system installed here would also have to consider the infrastructure problems more so than at T. These will have a significant effect on lead times.

Both T and N are examples of the types of management problems encountered in industry in a developing country. They provide examples of how the international manager involved with such situations needs to resolve management problems differently than in a U.S. environment.

SOME ADDITIONAL THOUGHTS

Are all the needs, goals, and problems that exist in Mexican or Indonesian manufacturing facilities similar to those of counterpart manufacturers in the United States? Of course not! So, why do the United States managers install systems that emphasize labor costing, labor efficiency, and production standards within environments that are trying to keep citizens employed?

Reflecting back on the "Shouldn'ts" of chapter 3, we find that many apply when analyzing systems for developing countries. Let's take a second look at the Shouldn'ts of American management as they relate to foreign environments.

1. The U.S. *shouldn't* assume that all similar businesses or plants are run the same or that all people and markets can be negotiated with in the same way. N and T do not fit this U.S. mold.
2. The U.S. *shouldn't* assume that it has the best production method for everyone. Asia and the Eastern Bloc offer some interesting ideas that may possibly work much better in developing countries.
3. The U.S. *shouldn't* set itself up as the world's instructor; rather, it should play the role of student if it wants to be better. The lessons that Japan has taught us should remind us of that, and there are many other teachers all around the world.
4. The U.S. *shouldn't* assume that Japan just has one small trick up its sleeve and that if we learn it we will be as good as we once were or even better. As long as we are playing catch-up, caught-up is all the better we'll get. The Koreans and other Asian countries are already looking beyond the goal of catching up to the Japanese.
5. The U.S. *shouldn't* assume that Japan is the best or only model to learn from. There are many models, some of which are much better in specific situations. The Japanese model won't work for T or N any better than the U.S. model.
6. The U.S. *shouldn't* work on the assumption that one method is good for everyone (MRP for the U.S. and JIT for Japan). The model selected for T will probably not be the best model for N, or vice versa.
7. The U.S. *shouldn't* assume that there is only one "best" model for running a factory, one best model for running a wholesale establish-

ment, one best model for running a retail establishment, etc. There are many models, many of which have appropriate applications in various environments. As this chapter demonstrates, the United States model would not work best for developing countries.

8. The U.S. *shouldn't* plan to lose its industry and be strictly a service society. Who wants to learn from a country that only teaches but can't be successful at what it teaches? Developing countries want to learn from countries that successfully practice what they preach.

9. The U.S. *shouldn't* live by the assumption that by managing only one of the three strategic resources—(1) materials, (2) labor, or (3) machinery, equipment, or facilities—it will manage all.

In developing countries, manufacturing facilities such as T and N need to establish company goals and objectives before a management or production control system is selected. For example, the U.S. assumes that its "get rich" philosophy appeals to everyone, whereas in the case of T, family time is more important than money. Consideration needs to be given to (this is only a partial list):[1]

1. Location of plant
2. Resource differences
   - Energy
   - Land availability
   - Infrastructure
3. Market differences
   - Traveling distances
   - Tariffs and quotas
4. Management expertise
5. Economic potential
   - Country
   - Company
6. Work force
   - Education
   - Motivation
   - Goals
7. Availability of machinery
   - Levels of automation
8. Inventory
   - Problems with inventory sources
   - Lead times
   - Financing costs
9. National goals and guidelines

---

[1]This list also applies to the United States or any other country. This emphasizes some of the differences between the United States and developing countries.

For example, in reference to N, the problem of blending high-tech engineering, no factory-floor automation, and an excess work force that is idle much of the time frustrates traditional production management philosophies. However, this is necessary when trying to satisfy the goals of the nation as well as those of the company.

Once we have evaluated the climate of a particular production or management environment, how do we develop an appropriate system? A unique system can be developed for each new environment, but this isn't always practical. However, if we realize that *every* country of the world was a developing country at some time, then we realize that it is appropriate to look at countries that have already developed production systems under conditions similar to the country under study. (This should be one of the primary applications of this book.)

Referring again to N or T, we see the need for a system that will work under conditions of:

For T
- No factory-floor automation
- Limited paperwork
- High worker-manager interface
- Over-employment
- A restrictive union

For N
- Poor infrastructure
- High technology in engineering
- No factory-floor automation
- Limited paperwork
- High worker-manager interface

By looking for a management system that satisfies these and other needs, a smoother-operating, more effective plant will be the result.

When planning for an appropriate production system, some industries require industry-specific production control systems. Process manufacturing plants are not run the same as discrete manufacturing plants, and so an industry-specific system should be implemented.

For developing countries, a few additional considerations should be mentioned. Some were evident in the T and N examples.

Infrastructure systems will most likely need improvement. Roadways, schools, electricity, water systems, and housing should not only be looked at from the company's perspective, but also from the community's perspective. This is the best—and many times the only—way to "sell" the company to the people. Don't expect the people to automatically like the plant. They aren't just sitting around waiting for you to give them a chance to work, and they often consider companies as intruders that are trying to take advantage of them. However, if a company is their friend rather than their exploiter, working with the people is much easier, and many extra costs involved will turn out to be minimal when compared to the benefits of improved relations with employees. Additionally, the government will love the company because it has created jobs for people who are working on the infrastructure systems.

Governmental relations are critical. Investigate the structure and procedures within the "system." It is important to work with the systems and not fight with the individuals in power. They should be given the respect that is due. If you treat them as bureaucratic nuisances, they'll recognize your attitude and treat you accordingly.

Border-crossing considerations are important in materials sourcing and product shipments. The distribution process is often critical to the product's effectiveness. Additionally, acquiring spare parts will be important in keeping machinery operational.

Search for local trends and attitudes and maintain harmony with them. One good way of doing this is by utilizing as few "foreigners" as possible in the factory. Foreigners are often considered intruders. When they are brought in, they should always have a local "advisor" on hand to make sure that consistency with local thought and traditions are maintained. The Japanese follow this policy when they install a factory in the United States, an environment with which they are familiar.

Find technology that is "appropriate" for the local environment, not technology that is "familiar" to the manager. This includes management methods, production methods, and the types of machines that are selected. Work within the limitations of the assumptions that have been established.

Develop appropriate measures of performance. Measure those areas that will motivate the labor force using their own goals and standards, not ours.

Individual performance standards are degrading and humiliating to many cultures, and only help to alienate workers. Team or company-wide performance standards may be much more effective. Additionally, the front-office, authoritarian-management style tends to alienate. A more participative, involved, walk-around management style develops a relationship between the employer and employee. The visibility of management is important in many cultures, even if it seems like a waste of time to the managers; it builds a binding and lasting relationship and will help to avoid confrontations.

The amount of time the employee of a developing country facility should spend in training will typically be much higher than that of his United States counterpart. Several months per year is not uncommon. This training should include areas that reach far beyond the scope of the company itself, such as personal health, first aid, construction skills, driving skills, cooking, sewing, sanitation systems, water purification, and so on. The training process will also help in the evaluation and selection of individuals who are natural leaders and who should be used as foremen and supervisors in the plant.

The installation of a management system or factory in a foreign environment must not be considered a short-term, money-making project. It must be looked at with a long-term perspective since that is the way the host population will view it.

I recommend reading *Small Is Beautiful* by Schumacher (Perennial Library, 1975) to get a clearer perspective of how a developing country perceives the United States. The only image many workers have of the United States comes from television shows such as "Dallas," "Knots Landing," and Clint Eastwood's Dirty Harry movies. A better understanding of their view of the U.S. can only help in the development of good relationships.

There is much literature that deals with the transfer of technology to developing countries. The World Bank is doing extensive research in this area, and an article by Dahlman and Westphal is a good summary of some of this work. In this article, they emphasize that, on many occasions, a modification to existing technology may be more advantageous than bringing in the "latest ideas" from the West. They also emphasize that there is not one best way for a country to adapt technology. Appropriate methods of adaptation should be investigated. The final sentence of this article says it best:

> The only recipe for success [in transferring technology to a developing country] is pragmatism based on constant monitoring of performance and of the possibilities opened up by new technological developments.[2]

More detailed information is available in a book published by the World Bank. Some of the key lessons for developing countries discussed in the Dahlman, Ross-Larson, and Westphal book cited at the end of this chapter include:

1. Targeting markets through the combined efforts of the government, industry, and the unions is valuable. This may include some protectionism while the industry is still in its infant stages within the country. In the long run, protectionism should be removed since its removal promotes technological development and makes the industry more competitive.
2. The selection of target markets should emphasize industries that have a strong export potential.
3. Technological strength is not that important in the early stages of industrial development, but expertise in the newly learned production process is. As long as the industry is in its early growth stages, becoming the best at what it's doing is the most important goal. Later, in order to become a major international contender, technological development and innovation becomes more important.
4. Short-term relationships with other countries and other companies are the most effective ways to learn about the products and production processes of a targeted industry.

[2]Dahlman, Carl and Larry Westphal, "The Transfer of Technology," *Finance and Development*, Dec. 1983, Vol. 20, #4, pp. 6-9.

5. Educational and training programs are vital to long-run success. These may include enticing nationals who are living and working in developed countries. These individuals can be brought "home" to manage and teach the growing industries of the country.

The World Bank is also a resource in many other areas that may be of interest to the reader. The articles it publishes can be acquired for a minimal cost. The following are examples of its research papers:

Appropriate Industrial Technology, Reference Nos. 671-51 and 671-77. This is a research paper on industrial development and the choice of appropriate technology.

The Industrial Incentive System in Morocco, Reference No. 671-85. This study reviews governmental influences in the form of industrial incentives.

"Shelter Strategies for the Urban Poor in Developing Countries," *Research Observer*, July 1986, Vol. 1, #2, pp. 183-203. This article reviews governmental policy and the development and construction of housing for the poor.

From Migrants to Proletarians: Employment Experience, Mobility, and Wages in Tanzania, World Bank Reprint Series: No. 250. This article discusses the use of incentives and the experiences of labor mobility in a developing country.

From these examples, it is easy to see that the World Bank is involved in many aspects of industrial management in developing countries. It is easy to get on their mailing list for *Research News*, a quarterly magazine that reviews current areas of research. Write to:

The World Bank
Headquarters
1818 H Street, NW
Washington, DC 20433

All countries are not alike. Many of the basic assumptions about management styles and techniques are not transferable, as the article by Partridge emphasizes. He lists several reasons, the key one being that the management personnel sent to foreign operations are not up to par with their United States counterparts. They know what the home office wants and how to run the operations, but they lack familiarity with the details and may not have anyone whom they can telephone to help them out. So, they do the best they can.

Couple the lack of experience cited by Partridge with the fact that the foreign environment isn't really conducive to United States methods, and we have an overabundance of struggling overseas plants, just like T and N. Fortunately, steps are being taken to improve management growth in developing countries, as cited in the article by Wallace. He suggests we emphasize four tactics to improve the effectiveness of management:

1. Program design which includes setting targets and measuring progress
2. The promotion and publicity of successful managers to raise their expectations
3. Dialogues with the manager
4. Incentive programs for the manager

These areas are emphasized by Wallace because he sees the developing-country manager as an isolated and forgotten individual. Wallace suggests programs that will bring this manager back into the limelight. Based on my experience, I would add these requirements for successful developing-country management: The manager must have more freedom in the decision-making process and must be flexible enough to adapt to the circumstances he is facing. The home office is often ignorant of the struggles faced by the foreign manager, and as such, they should let him have the freedom to manage his problems as he sees fit, not as the home office dictates.

In summary, the basic assumptions upon which we develop a management or production system for a particular country will rarely fit the United States model. We must look for more flexible methods in order to find solutions that will be more appropriate than those we have at home. We must be receptive to systems that can be adapted to these environments. Only by utilizing more appropriate systems will the host population, management, and the production facility be able to maximize their benefits.

REFERENCES

Bell, Martin, Bruce Ross-Larson, and Larry E. Westphal. *Assessing the Performance Of Infant Industries*, World Bank Staff Working Papers, No. 666, throughout September 1984.

Dahlman, Carl J., Bruce Ross-Larson, and Larry E. Westphal. *Managing Technological Development—Lessons From Newly Industrializing Countries*, World Bank Staff Working Papers, No. 717, January 1985.

Dahlman, Carl J. and Larry E. Westphal. "The Transfer Of Technology," *Finance & Development*, December 1983, Vol. 20, #4, pp. 6-9.

Khandwalla, Pradip N. "Turnaround Management Of Mismanaged Complex Organizations," *International Studies Of Management And Organization*, Winter 1983-1984, Vol. 13, #4, pp. 5-41.

Partridge, Simon. "Why Management Won't Transfer," *Management Today*, July 1980, pp. 25-26.

Plenert, Gerhard J. "Getting The Best Of Technology Transfer," *P&IM Review*, Volume 5, No. 3, March 1985.

———. "Production Considerations In Developing Countries," *Proceedings Of The 28th Annual International Conference Of The American Production And Inventory Control Society*, 1985.

Schumacher, E.F. *Small is Beautiful—Economics as if People Mattered* New York, Perennial Library, 1975.

Sinha, Jai B.P. "A Model Of Effective Leadership Styles In India," *International Studies Of Management And Organization*, Summer/Fall 1984, Vol. 14, #2-3, pp. 86-98.

Solomon, Stephen D. "Where In The World Is Pittsburg, Anyway," *Inc.*, Jan. 1985, Vol. 7, #1, pp. 58-66.

Wallace, John B. "Fostering Management Growth In Developing Countries," *Training And Development Journal*, Jan. 1985, pp. 67-73.

11

Reflecting Back

A consultant was on an information-gathering expedition and was interviewing a middle-management employee about the management style of his company. Most of the manager's comments were negative, beginning with, "Management does this," or, "Management expects that." The consultant asked him how he defined the term *management* and he responded, "That's simple. Management is everybody above me!"

It's easy to relate to the manager in this story. Many of us have often felt that way. Sometimes it's difficult to realize that if we want something changed, we're the ones that will have to do the changing.

Reflecting back on chapter 1 where the goal of this book was presented, we can now review how this goal was achieved. The goal is:

To help the management of United States industry become more competitive in manufacturing facilities both in the United States and overseas.

To achieve this goal, we have examined 30 countries, searching for management systems that would be of interest to United States managers. Most of these are positive, usable systems that can be implemented in U.S. facilities. A few countries (for example, Cuba) provided negative examples and were included as a warning so that we don't make the same mistakes.

Two developing countries were also examined to teach the "international manager" about differences in the styles of developing-country management. This reinforces a lesson:

Regardless of how similar two factories may be in the products they produce or in the manufacturing techniques they use, if they are located in different countries, they will require different management styles.

This book provides a multitude of ideas for United States managers, that are summarized in CHART 11.1. Many may initially seem far-fetched or inappropriate, but that's what American automobile manufacturers initially said about the Japanese methods of manufacturing. Let's look at two areas that were claimed as being "impossible" in the United States (these are taken from chapter 6).

Lifetime vendors.[1] In order to deliver parts, such vendors are often required, under this philosophy, to have their facilities close to the automobile manufacturers they serve. Initially, United States automakers consider this "impossible;" they felt they couldn't force vendors to move their facilities.

The Japanese came along and proposed building a major manufacturing facility in the Kentucky/Tennessee area. They promised their vendors long-term supplier contracts if they would locate themselves within a couple hours driving time from the manufacturing facility. Some suppliers fought this idea, but it was no problem for the Japanese to come up with alternative suppliers in those cases. The facility now exists and operates using the initially rejected Japanese concept of lifetime vendors.

Morale programs.[2] As part of this program, employees take occasional rest and stretch breaks. This idea seemed ridiculous to United States auto manufacturers and was never considered as a viable technique. However, a tour of the Japanese-managed manufacturing facility in Fremont, California shows that even Americans can jog and do jumping jacks during their rest breaks.

All the ideas mentioned in this book are worthy of further investigation and possible implementation. Remember, there is no "correct" or "perfect" way to manage any facility.

Take, for example, self-management. This is being attempted in several industries in the United States, but with limited success. Several of these attempts have already met with defeat. Perhaps the first step in such a venture should not be *totally* dependent upon American ingenuity (as valuable as it is); Yugoslavia and Israel provide successes and failures in the development of self-management operations. These countries must have learned some concepts over their years of experience that would be of value to us.

Another example is found in participative management. The article by Kelly and Khozan cited at the end of this chapter suggests that Europe is far ahead of the United States. Previous efforts to transfer participative management ideas to the United States from such places as the Volvo plant in Sweden have been unsuccessful; the high level of resistance tends to crush the system's effectiveness. So, why is it successful in Europe? What can we change to make it valu-

---

[1] A detailed explanation of this concept can be found in chapter 6.

[2] A detailed explanation of this concept can be found in chapter 6.

able to us? Are there situations where it would indeed be more valuable than what we are currently doing? For now, it looks like participative management will eventually need to be a tool in the United States.

Even a country as vastly different from the United States as the Soviet Union has lessons for us and for developing countries. The Soviet Union is pushing hard for technological growth and mechanization and for the work force to increase its educational level. What has been discovered, though, is that there aren't enough people interested in doing the trivial, menial jobs, such as farm work. Additionally, the newly educated work force can't find enough satisfying jobs. What this imbalance has created is a job market with low productivity, insufficient jobs, and a shortage of workers.

The Soviets are trying to resolve this problem by using incentive systems with good pay to motivate the workers. The use of Worker Brigades helps to develop a friendly environment for the worker and makes work more interesting. With the proper balance and incentives, the current imbalance of needs can be corrected. This illustration from the Soviet Union teaches the international manager some valuable lessons about motivating workers in developing countries.

Another tool for achieving this book's goal of helping managers become more competitive is that it offers a better understanding of foreign competition. For example, chapter 8 examines the eagerness that countries like South Korea have for a share of United States markets and outlines what product areas are being targeted.

Still another tool (see chapter 1) of importance to United States managers is the need to "internationalize" them by offering them alternatives for management problems. As a result, a variety of solutions can be generated. For example, the production scheduling system used for production control in a factory can be labor-oriented (MRP in the United States and Europe), materials-oriented (JIT in Japan), or equipment/facilities-oriented (OPT in Israel).[3]

An extension of this is the concept fostered by Robert T. Moran (cited at the end of this chapter), that of "cultural synergy." He describes this as the blending of two business cultures in order to develop a third. Moran suggests taking the best business-management system tool of each culture and developing a third that performs better for both. He also supports the idea that Japan is not the only source of ideas for management models. In his article, he lists some techniques that he considers worth adapting from Europe, most of which are included in my list in some form, and suggests ways of implementing some of these in the United States.

United States industry *can* become more competitive in its manufacturing facilities, and the ideas in this book can help tremendously in achieving this goal. Use CHART 11.1 as a summary of ideas or an index to this book. As you look for

---

[3]Chapter 2 offers a detailed explanation of how these systems developed and how they differ.

Chart 11.1. Recapping the Countries

Country	Assumptions	Goals	Production Methods	Management Tools	Organization Style	Personnel-Management Style
United States	Excessive land space Low interest rates (now invalid)	Labor efficiency Balanced factory Profits	Push production systems such as MRP EOQ for materials planning	Efficiency reporting and control	Top-down	Domineering
Japan	Limited land space Long distance to markets Importation of raw materials and energy Improvement-oriented Simplification Automation Innovations Diversity	Minimize materials High quality Full employment Internationally competitive	Facilities planning • Shared resources • Smaller factories • Technical specialization Production planning • Production sequencing • In-line quality control • Just-in-time or KANBAN • Split shifts • Lifetime vendors	Management circles Bottom-up management Statistical management Long-run planning	Bottom-up	Passive Lifetime employment No nepotism Profit bonuses Morale programs Employee rotation
Israel	Limited land space High intellectual level High inflation rates Importation of raw materials and energy Political isolation Long distance from international markets	Economic efficiency Profitability Research and development orientation	Centrally managed (like OPT)	Kibbutz Self-management	Worker participation	Participative Prestrike worker sanctions Labor mediation

Latin America (common traits)	High debt level Governmental influences are important	Full employment Competitive in world market	Learning by doing Technological information centers Technological adaptability Sunrise industry support	Education (including the basics)
Puerto Rico	Culturally diverse Outside influences Dominance by U.S.			Value employees highly Nonparticipation of employees
Argentina	High inflation		Adaptability	
Brazil				
Mexico			Transfer of technology	
Canada	High production costs Low productivity Source of raw materials Dependency on other countries	Small-business emphasis International markets	Specialization	Hazardous waste treatment Research-sharing Emphasis on quality over quantity
Europe (common traits)	Cultural synergy	International orientation	Long-term planning Authoritarian style Less concentration of power in any one individual	Board of managers do decision-making Organizational structure less rigid than in U.S. Social and human relations perspective Job rotation and orientation programs Indexation of labor wages

Chart 11.1. Continued

Country	Assumptions	Goals	Production Methods	Management Tools	Organization Style	Personnel-Management Style
Europe (common traits)						Fewer titles and "elite" management slots
Belgium			Specialization			Personnel motivation
Finland			Periodic production control Management circle—project groups Flexibility in manufacturing			
France				Socialistic perspective on authority		
Ireland			Modern production systems			
Netherlands			Research on P&IC (production and inventory control) systems Flexible work systems in assembly			
Norway			High-tech manufacturing	Decentralization		Industrial democracy Work environment reform

Spain						Workplace democracy
Sweden	Socialistic, Strong unions, Single culture			Management/worker codetermination		Worker motivation
Switzerland	Landlocked	Industrial research	Hazards management, Consolidation, Quality, Consistency			
United Kingdom		International marketing				Labor strains—10 to 15 unions per factory, Labor relations programs, Workplace democracy
West Germany	Blend of cultures			Decentralized management, Employee "think tanks", Less of a workload planned per time period	Worker/shareholder decision-sharing, Codetermination	Flex time, Worker allegiance to company and not just to union
Asia (common traits)						Relationship-oriented performance appaisals
China (PRC)	Large population, Domineering government, Centrally managed pricing	Strong family ties		Communes	Worker-controlled enterprises	Quota systems and bonuses, Governmental unions

Chart 11.1. Continued

Country	Assumptions	Goals	Production Methods	Management Tools	Organization Style	Personnel-Management Style
Hong Kong	No governmental support Turnover to PRC in 1997		"Hot" product orientation Plant staging for PRC			
India	Cultural/religious resistance to change Enormous population Heavy agriculture			Entrepreneur training programs	Joint worker councils	Importance of personal relationships
Singapore	Strong government support of industry High living standards International dependence on technology High dependence on trade		High-tech orientation			
South Korea	Strong drive Debtor nation	Push for technological independence	Technological selectivity High R&D reinvestment			Nepotism Education abroad Hiring employees from abroad
Taiwan	Confucianism Shortage of educational facilities Rich government with many programs Governmental incentives		Technological development Many small "family" companies			Worker-employer relationship most important Emphasis on interdependence of employees

Reflecting Back

Eastern Bloc Countries (common traits)	Slow economic growth Trade deficits Inflation	Movement towards pricing system guideposts Movement towards decentralized planning Movement towards use of the market		Central planning	Move towards autonomy of individual enterprise	Incentive systems
Cuba	Pricing structure			Moral Economy Dropped Moral Economy for economic incentives		
Czechoslovakia	Low productivity	Basic needs—fuel, housing, etc.	High-tech firms			
Poland	Balance of trade deficit		Housing cooperatives	Interest in MBO	Independent Western enterprises	Solidarity
Soviet Union	Out of touch with populace Highly agricultural	Shift towards need for consumer goods	Central planning model	Training for managers	Worker brigades	"Inventors and innovators"
Yugoslavia	Removal of central planning		Decentralization	Worker enterprise management	BOALs—Workers' councils Enterprise autonomy	
Turkey	Leadership push for rapid growth and development Field-to-factory migration				Blend of state and private enterprises	

new ideas, refer to it. If something appears appropriate, review the chapter that discusses the technique and you are on your way to a solution.

Also, refer to chapter 10 when looking at a business or factory in a developing country; it has many good dos and don'ts.

REFERENCES

Kelly, Joe and Kamran Khozan. "Participative Management: Can It Work?" *Business Horizons*, August 1980, pp. 74-79.

Moran, Robert T. "Theory Z: But Not Japan," *S.A.M. Advance Management Journal*, Autumn 1983, pp. 27-33.

12

What's Happening in the United States?

A little boy lived in a small remote town in the western part of China. He had heard stories told about the great insight and wisdom of a sage that lived in a cave near the top of the mountain close to his home. Feeling that he was pretty wise himself, the little boy thought he would test the sage's wisdom. He caught a tiny sparrow and climbed the mountain to visit the wise man. As he entered the cave, he held the sparrow in his hands behind his back so the sage couldn't see what he had.

The little boy then asked, "I hold a sparrow in my hands. Tell me, is it alive or is it dead?"

The sage, knowing that the boy planned to trick him, responded, "Little boy, in your hands you hold the power of life or death. You have the power to kill the bird or to let it live just to prove me wrong. Use that power wisely. Use it to gain wisdom, not to test my patience."

How often do we fall into the trap of trying to disprove someone else's wisdom? Our time would be much better spent if we used our time to increase our own wisdom. To do this, we should first look for strengths upon which the United States can build.

Get a map of the world and look at the north-central region of California. In this area you will find a long green patch called the Sacramento Valley. Now, look at Asia, including Japan, China, Thailand, Malaysia, Indonesia, and all the other countries, and consider this—more rice is grown in the Sacramento Valley than in all of Asia.[1]

---

[1]This is difficult to specifically document because of the complexity of getting data out of China. However, the difference is enough to prove my point without specific numbers.

Next, look at the Eastern Bloc nations: the Soviet Union (south-western region), East Germany, Poland, Czechoslovakia, Romania, Yugoslavia, and all the others. Less than 100 years ago, this region used to feed the entire continent. Today, it can't even feed itself. It depends on the United States and Canada for certain foods.

WORLD AGRICULTURAL SUPERIORITY

Case in point—*the United States has world agricultural superiority in unbelievable proportions.*

A second dominating strength of the United States is found by asking the question, What organization develops more technology than any other in the world? Not just a little more, but a *lot* more than anyone else in the world. While some readers can guess the answer fairly quickly, we'll leave it for now.

Factory floor automation has received a recent surge of interest. Companies like General Electric, IBM, and Westinghouse are playing the roles of both vendor and user of these hi-tech systems. Buzzwords like JIT, CAD/CAM, robotics, and CIM (computer integrated manufacturing) are hot in the business world. The goal is to design a product on a CAD terminal and have that design technology transferred directly to the factory floor (CAM). There, computerized automatic inventory picking and receiving systems bring in the parts necessary for manufacturing. Robots select the appropriate parts and the appropriate machine tools to do the job.

Production scheduling is carried out by the CIM system which incorporates MRP for purchasing parts and JIT for scheduling on the factory floor. Once scheduled, Automatic Guided Vehicle systems pick the parts from the Automatic Picking and Retrieving systems and deliver them to robots on the factory floor. These robots then produce the needed parts on the CAM-integrated production machinery.[2]

LARGEST PRODUCER OF TECHNOLOGY

Now, let's answer the question that was left hanging—*the largest producer of technology in the world is the United States government.* Here's an even bigger question. Who is the largest user (more appropriately called "adapter") of this U.S. government-developed technology in the world (other than the U.S. government)? Again, you may be left hanging for a moment.

United States businesses place very little effort on adapting the existing United States government technology. This is in spite of the fact that this technology is absolutely free to anyone who requests it. Often, industry will research and resolve a problem that has already been solved by some govern-

---

[2]The West Europeans (West Germany, Sweden, and Switzerland) and Czechoslovakians know a few things we could learn in the area of factory-floor automation.

ment agency simply because management didn't bother to check on what was available. Using previously developed technology can avoid extensive duplication and can reduce development time by as much as 50 percent, if only industry would take the time to look.[3] This lack of interest by U.S. industry for government technology demonstrates the lack of a technologically adaptive management style (several examples of adaptive management are seen in Latin America). Since we have identified technology as one of our biggest strengths, industrial managers should learn to become more efficient at using resources that already exist.

To answer the hanging question, the largest user of United States government-developed technology, outside of the government itself, is the Soviet Union. Since copies of the technology are readily available, the Soviets make sure they have plenty of copies. If you're a U.S. citizen, doesn't this make you feel like your tax dollars are being put to good use?

NEEDED CHANGES

Having looked at two strengths of the United States—agriculture and technology—let's take a closer look to see why it is losing its competitive edge by focusing now on weaknesses. Two choice industrial examples are the automobile and electronics industries. General Motors, Ford, and Chrysler are all struggling to regain their market share. Up to now, the competition has been coming from Japan, but soon Korea will be making major inroads as well. Yugoslavia is also trying to enter the U.S. marketplace.

---

[3]An entire network of people has been established to help United States industry tap into already-developed government technology. This network publishes literature on what is available, and has individuals whose sole function is to transfer government technology to private industry. Technology exists in all areas, from construction to robotics to a library of 1,600 computer programs. To tap into this resource, here are two sources:

The Technology Transfer Society
Suite 800 AIAA
9841 Airport Blvd.
Los Angeles, CA 90045

Dr. J. Jolly
TECTRA Newsletter
CSUS
School of Business
Sacramento, CA 95819

An excellent publication that will introduce you to technologies that are appropriate for adaptation or which have already been adapted into industry is *NASA Tech Briefs*. This can be ordered free of charge by writing to:

NASA STI Facility
Manager, TU Division
P.O. Box 8757
Baltimore, MD 21240-0757

What's Happening in the United States?

In the electronics industry, Japan has already captured a major portion. Japan plans to increase its share of the U.S. electronics industry market, and South Korea, Taiwan, and Singapore hope to take major portions of the market as well.

A few of the significant areas where numerous foreign examples exist that can benefit the United States in particular include:

1. Short-term financial goals
2. Worker motivation
3. Labor "babysitting"
4. Hi-tech blindness
5. Who's management?
6. Authoritarianism
7. Three-part harmony
8. Flexibility and adaptability
9. Know the customer; know the competitor

Short-term Financial Goals

The time perspective of American management is very shortsighted. Stockholders want annual profits. They elect boards of directors who vote for short-term profit goals. The boards, in turn, select managers who will promise them annual profits. As a result, the management of the companies look for short-term, quick-return projects that will satisfy these demands. Managers use this as their directive when they approve projects that minimize capital outlays. In other words, since it is cheaper to repair an old piece of junk than it is to replace it (in the short run), we patch rather than replace.

Japan's success has often been excused with the argument that, after World War II, it was forced to build new factories with new equipment, whereas in the United States we had to continue working on our old equipment. This argument holds little weight when we realize that the Japanese have already replaced most of their post-World War II equipment, while the United States is still running on pre-World War II equipment.

The price the U.S. pays for its short-term profit mentality is inefficiency, low productivity, and higher inventories that have to be financed at higher rates of interest. The Japanese and the Koreans quickly took advantage of this weakness.

Solutions for short-term thinking can be found by studying other countries for new ideas. In this case, a feasible option is found in Japan which encourages companies to have a larger proportion of debt-to-equity financing. This means that the banks or financing organizations own larger portions of the companies than do the stockholders. By doing this, it is assumed that the financing organizations are more prone to look at long-term returns than short-term profits. The organizations are owned primarily by stockholders (the financing organizations) who realize the advantages of allowing these organizations to run their industries with a long-term perspective in mind.

Worker Motivation

Worker motivation is lacking in United States plants. Our teachers of management techniques tell us that status symbols or recognition are better motivators than pay increases or promotions. Reread the Cuban example if you believe this nonsense. Recognition motivators work only as long as they are new, but after a few years they are taken lightly by the workers.

Many companies and other countries have picked up on the worker-team concept. This encourages the workers to motivate each other and makes them feel more in control of their destiny. In many cases, such teams are even self-managing.

Labor "Babysitting"

This term is used to describe the U.S. obsession with employee efficiency reporting. We make studies of every movement that a worker makes, making sure that he sneezes efficiently, but we don't seem to take notice of the enormous pile of inventory sitting in front of his workstation. This inventory is setting there to ensure that the employee has plenty of work to do so that he can be efficient. Unfortunately, the financing costs on this inventory are too high to be justifiable.

Labor cost now averages only about 7 to 12 percent of the total cost of a manufactured product. A 1-percent improvement in this area (.07 to .12 percent improvement overall) is not nearly as effective as a one-percent improvement in the remaining 88 to 93 percent (.88 to .93 percent overall). Many companies have realized this difference and are downplaying labor-oriented management styles.

In adopting a nonlabor management style, many countries have installed systems to monitor teams of workers and to measure team performance rather than individual performance. The members of the team motivate each other, since the team as a whole will receive bonuses.

Hi-Tech Blindness

To understand this term, let's look at the recent surge of microcomputer purchases, and how these high sales have suddenly dropped off. It is estimated that about one-third of the microcomputers purchased for businesses are actually being used for the purpose for which they were purchased. The other two-thirds are either not being used properly or are not being used at all.

Recent literature has attempted to indoctrinate us to think that information is the wave of the future. It is believed that the more information we have, the better off we will be. This may be true in specific cases, such as for making forecasts, but it certainly isn't true for everything. For example, for production control in an automobile factory, the United States uses elaborate computer systems to generate its MRP schedules. At the same time, Japan uses no computer to schedule its JIT production control systems. New automotive factories now tend to avoid the hi-tech MRP solution and instead install the simple and dumb JIT system.

Piles of reports are distributed throughout the factory. Managers have to have "status symbol" reports delivered to them weekly or even daily. How many are really used or are necessary?

It is important to realize that the United States is about the only country in the world that is obsessed with the "information age"; most others are looking for simplification rather than automation, and consider less paperwork an improvement over more information.

A variety of solutions to this problem are found in other countries. Industrial "focusing" in many Asian countries helps companies stress growth in specific directions that are internationally marketable. Europe embodies multinational agreements where the technology centers of these countries aim their technology at specific, internationally marketable products. This "focusing" is something that is lacking in the United States environment and finds us getting overly wrapped-up in the glamour of hi-tech while at the same time forgetting the direction or purpose of the technology. This lack of focus also extends to the "information society." The obsession with having as much information as possible has camouflaged the basic principle that needs to be established, and that is, "What specific question will be answered by the acquisition of this piece of information?" If there is no specific use for it, why acquire it?

I once visited a factory, and as my host and I drove towards it, we passed a pile of gravel. In the gravel was stuck a sign that read, "Caution: Pile of Gravel."

I asked, "Why is that pile of gravel there?"

My host looked at the pile, then at me somewhat confused, and responded, "I don't know, I guess it's there to hold up the sign!"

This reminds me of situations where piles of gravel (systems) are installed to hold up signs (to solve problems) that wouldn't have existed if it weren't for the piles. Are we generating information or piles of gravel with signs?

Be on your guard against hi-tech blindness. Put this slogan on your wall— "It is better to eliminate than to automate." The simpler a task is, the easier and cheaper it will run. Too often, we let "paralysis through analysis" occur by performing endless studies that go nowhere and only eat up time and money.

Who's Management?

This idea is demonstrated in the story at the beginning of chapter 11 about the middle manager who said, "Management is everybody above me." There needs to be an awakening of conscious responsibility. Business needs to realize that if anything is to be changed, it's up to each manager individually to make the change. Unless we get involved in this change, it won't happen. Out of this have sprung the worker participation management styles of many other countries. In Yugoslavia, West Germany, India and many other countries, some form of this system exists. In some countries, the workers act as advisors, and in other countries, the worker has an equal say in the management of the company.

Information should flow top-down and management should flow bottom-up, never the other way around. Information about corporate goals, guidelines, programs, and problems should be shared with the workers so they can be a more effective part of the organization. Workers *cannot* support management's efforts and direction if they are kept uninformed.

At the same time, we need to let workers and supervisors make as many decisions as possible. They know best how to do their jobs, so higher levels of management have to let them do it. The more "guidelines" and "directives" lower-level management is given, the more they will be afraid to make their own decisions.

Authoritarianism

Our authoritarian style of management exists in very few other countries. Worker councils, worker brigades, quality circles, management circles, participative management, and other similar concepts have taken the place of authoritarianism. For these management styles to be effective, they need more than a suggestion box-style of management. The workers' ideas must be implemented for the flow of ideas to continue. Experience in other countries shows that management overrides on more than five percent of the ideas will discourage the workers' participation.

I was touring a factory in the eastern U.S. when I asked the factory manager, "About how many people work here."

His response was significant. He said, "About half."

Using this manager's response and reviewing CHART 11.1 for areas where the United States may be lacking, attention is immediately drawn to the need for us to work harder in the area of personnel relations and personnel management. This isn't to say that many positive things aren't happening. For example, the article by Marth cited at the end of this chapter discusses how 3M's Chairman and CEO encourages and promotes an open-door policy for all his employees, even factory-floor workers. Unfortunately, though, this is not widespread.

Let's look at some statistics for further understanding. A survey was recently taken by the Institute of Industrial Engineers (IIE). The report is titled *Productivity Today: A Summary of the Fifth Annual Productivity Survey Con-*

ducted by the Institute of Industrial Engineers.[4] In this survey, 47.6 percent of the respondents felt that the attitudes of those who worked in their companies were not very enthusiastic or optimistic. In other words, management felt that employee attitude is quite negative.

Another question asked in this report was, What is the most effective way to encourage people to offer ideas to improve productivity? Of the respondents, 58.6 percent felt that personal recognition was more effective than money or promotion. Reread the section on Cuba or Japan if you believe this nonsense. Sure, personal recognition is important, but you better tie money or a promotion to it too or else you're not going to get a long-term, meaningful change in worker attitudes.

Another statistic that was interesting is that 71.2 percent of the respondents felt that in the next 10 years, at least one other country will be more productive than the United States and that we will have lost our ranking as the most productive nation in the world.

This raises several questions. First, is there a relationship between productivity and labor relations techniques? The answer is, "Yes!" Refer to CHART 11.1 to see how many countries (including the Eastern Bloc) have formal incentive, employee relations, or employee-management participation programs.

The problem in the United States is not that we have low productivity, but that we have low productivity growth.[5] We have begun to stagnate. We are failing to motivate ourselves to achieve greater goals. Where does this drive for success come from? Our leaders, of course! If employee attitudes are poor, as the survey indicates, we shouldn't blame the workers but rather the motivators.

Who are the responsible motivators? Supervisors blame middle management. Middle management blames top management. Top management blames the United States Congress, and Congress blames the President. Let's face it

---

[4]The respondents were industrial engineers and managers. The survey publication mentioned has interesting information about the effectiveness of computers and production control methodologies. It can be ordered from:

IIE
25 Technology Park/Atlanta
Norcross, Georgia 30092
Phone: (404) 449-0460

[5]United States productivity growth in selected areas (percent per annum):

	1961/69	1970/73	1974/82
Output per person	2.5	1.4	0.1
Real GNP growth	4.4	3.6	1.9

Source: U.S. Department of Commerce.

though, we're all motivators. If we don't like something, it's our job to change it, not to complain about it.

Three-Part Harmony

Three-part harmony refers to the fact that the government, management, and union thrive on antagonizing each other. The government builds bureaucratic zoos to "keep business and unions in line." Unions consider themselves the conscience of management. Management in turn fights anything that comes from either the government or the unions, even if it would have been beneficial to agree.

The solution to this problem is buried in a much deeper problem, and reference is made once again to the book *Megatrends* to identify this problem. The book states that one of the trends for the future is a movement away from the family towards the individual. This is demonstrated by the increasing number of single-parent families and the high divorce rate. This is a large part of the reason for the lack of unity that exists in the United States. If we as individual citizens can't make one-on-one relationships work, we are not ready to make broader relationships work, and we will not be successful in uniting the government, management, and the unions. The solution to *national* unity is *individual* unity centered in the ability of individuals to work together on a one-on-one basis.

It has been said that the United States will change when it hurts enough to make change worthwhile. Hurt is the motivator that will pull unions, business, and the government together in a combined effort. This is a sad prediction for our future.

National industrial programs to improve unity exist in most countries. Here, the efforts of the nation are focused on certain problems or products. MITI of Japan is an excellent example of such an organization (see The Role of the Government in chapter 6). In MITI, the government sees itself as the servant of industry and looks for ways to help industry become better. In contrast, the United States government sees itself as the enforcer of business, making sure business stays in line. This makes our business community hesitant to work with the government. Without a change in attitude on both sides, a national industrial program will not work. *With* such a program, though, we could focus our technology and become more effective as an international competitor.

Flexibility and Adaptability

The sledgehammered implementation of any of the techniques described in this book is sure to bring failure. People affected by a system change need to understand what is being done and why. This way, they will support rather than oppose changes.

Adaptability also involves recognizing that it may be necessary to convince the appropriate union and legal authorities that a proposed change by management is indeed an improvement. Unfortunately, there have been cases where resistance to a change was so great that it became necessary to move the factory. This can be seen in the migration of factories out of the Detroit area where unions have become very powerful.

Flexibility and adaptability may require a change in processing procedures. For example, the Mexican cement manufacturer discussed in chapter 5 found it necessary to adapt his production methodologies to suit the climate and materials available locally for his facilities.

The United States has demonstrated its lack of flexibility in an obsession for labor-controlling management styles. (This was discussed in chapter 2.) The automobile industry has recently been forced to consider a less labor-oriented style, one that is more materials-management oriented. However, the accounting and costing structures still embody "standard costs" and efficiency ratings. To remove this bias and open the door for adapting a different manufacturing management style, three major changes must occur:

1. Eliminate costing systems
2. Eliminate financial analysis systems
3. Eliminate asset ratios

Both Japan and Israel have eliminated their costing systems in their JIT and OPT philosophies.[6] They consider the evaluation of individual performance as a deterrent to overall factory productivity. For them, the only meaningful cost number is the total cost of production. Recent studies on how to improve for outdated costing methods can be found in the Beliner and Brimson book listed at the end of this chapter.

Financial analysis has been eliminated by the Japanese because they view it as being too short-term oriented. This is, of course, a major difference between United States and Japanese management styles. Long-term project evaluation contains too many unknowns for an effective and meaningful financial evaluation to be performed. Even Japanese banks consider this form of evaluation worthless. Keeping in mind what we just discussed regarding short-term financial goals, we need to remember that the time perspective of future projects should be lengthened. Having expanded our scope to the long range, financial analysis is of little value.

Asset ratios are used to show the asset strength of a company. The larger the assets, the stronger the company. Unfortunately, these ratios ignore the fact that inventory is an asset, and that larger inventories, under this reasoning, would actually make a company look good. This is of course ridiculous, since financing these inventories increases product costs and makes a company less profitable. However, many plant managers in the United States have refused to

---

[6]See chapter 2 for a comparison of the United States MRP technique, the Japanese JIT technique, and the Israeli OPT technique. Additionally, chapter 6 discusses JIT and chapter 7 discusses OPT.

lower their inventories because it would destroy their asset ratios, which are more important to corporate than overall profit.

These three points—the elimination of costing, financial analysis, and asset ratios—would upset the accounting and financial communities if implemented. However, these are the most critical biases that need to be eliminated for adaptability to occur.

United States managers can improve their flexibility by, first of all, removing the biases mentioned in chapter 1, the most critical being that the United States way of doing things is not the only way, nor is it always the best way. Next, managers must open their minds to new ideas and look for ways of adapting these ideas into their existing operations.

None of the techniques described in this book should be considered as being unadaptable in the United States for social, political, or governmental reasons. They are *all* usable. Union and management biases are the only obstacles that would keep any of these techniques from being used. Of these two, the more rigid to change is management. Management tends to want to stay with what's comfortable rather than to make waves. From this resistance comes the saying "The hardest rocks (resistance to change) wear ties."

Know the Customer; Know the Competitor

The goals of the corporation should center around quality and customer satisfaction rather than revenues. With a quality product and happy customers, revenues become a by-product. The best way to beat our international competitors is to know a little more about the customers' needs than they do. We need to identify the needs of the customer and develop products that meet those needs. This sounds like a statement from a basic marketing text, and it is. Unfortunately, many products are developed without ever asking the customers what *they* want. The Concord is an excellent example of a multimillion-dollar investment in development that never considered the needs of the customer.

The second best way to beat our competitors is to know more about them than they know about us. This way, you can cash in on their weaknesses. Apple's knowledge of IBM's avoidance of the small-computer market helped it to get a big head start in the microcomputer industry.

Reflecting on current management problems isn't enough to rebuild our competitive edge. The United States has the best technology and agricultural resources in the world. We're highest in productivity and we offer more opportunities for industrial growth for the individual small enterprise than does any other nation. We should cash in on these advantages by setting *positive goals for the future*.

Currently, one of the most prominent and accepted predictors of the future of United States industry is *Megatrends*. This book foresees (based on current trends) the United States as losing its industry and becoming a service or information society, and that we are destined to service the rest of the world with our technology and management information.

Fortunately, there are those who don't agree with this prediction, claiming that the rest of the world doesn't want our self-acclaimed expertise. Other countries would rather get Japanese technology and learn about Japan's production methodologies. Which country would you rather learn from if you were going to manufacture cars, Japan or the U.S.?

Within the United States, there is little interest in becoming more dependent on the rest of the world. We've had enough experience with the oil crisis to realize that we don't want any more dependency. However, the movement of our factories overseas could create more OPEC-type problems.

The Japanese don't agree with the *Megatrends* prognosis that the United States should manufacture overseas where labor is cheaper. This is evident in that the Japanese are building more and more factories in the United States. They see our labor force as being competitive if treated properly, and they're willing to invest in us even if we aren't.

The United States has only lost the number one productivity slot if it gives up. Hopefully, that isn't what has happened to the 71.2 percent mentioned earlier in the IIE survey. We have plenty of tools to work with, including the strongest technological capability in the world. There are seven areas where these tools need to be applied:

1. *Schools.* The colleges and universities of the nations must modify their short-term quick-profit way of thinking. The new management styles discussed in this book need to be addressed.
2. *Business.* The business community needs to update its management philosophy in areas such as personnel management and motivation, short-sightedness, harmony, flexibility, and adaptability.
3. *Government.* The United States government needs to think of itself as the servant of business, not as its policeman. In turn, it will get more cooperation from the business world. Using the MITI organization in Japan as a role model may be a good start.
4. *Unions.* If unions would look to the needs of the business community rather than just at their own needs, business would be less hostile towards them.
5. *Financial community.* The financial community needs to recognize the rigidity it is creating, which is resulting in a lack of growth. Costing systems, asset ratios, and most financial analysis systems are obsolete. Additionally, a growth in debt financing is needed to remove short-term thinking.
6. *Churches.* In earlier times, the strength of the United States lay in the type of people that composed the country's population. These people looked for challenges and were not afraid of work. Today, many Americans try to avoid work. Many have lost the work ethic that at one time

made this a great country, and it is in the churches of the United States where the American worker needs to relearn this ethic. We need to relearn that dependency is not prosperity, whether it's the individual dependent on welfare or the nation dependent on OPEC.

The churches also need to teach ethics and integrity. Employees and business leaders need to be trustworthy and dependable if they want to build stronger working relationships with each other and with other countries.

7. *Individuals.* The search for unity and stronger one-on-one relationships will build the family and the organization. This area is the key to getting the other six areas of work together.

The goal of this book has been to help the United States manager become more competitive at home and abroad. This chapter offered a summary of ideas that will help to achieve this goal. Previous chapters detailed over a hundred tools that are available worldwide to help with this objective. We must remember that, as long as we play catch-up, the best we can do is get caught-up. We must take advantage of our strengths and move ahead of our foreign competitors. Let's not give up and take the role of an "information society." *We can get ahead* if we use proper planning, take advantage of our technological strengths to develop new ideas, get rid of our old management styles, and introduce new management techniques.

The great thing in this world is not so much where we stand, as in what direction we are moving.

Oliver Wendell Holmes

REFERENCES

Banks, Harold, "Holding For Takeoff," *Forbes*, June 20, 1983, Vol. 131, #13, pp. 50-54.

Berliner, Callie and James A. Brimson. *Cost Management for Today's Advanced Manufacturing—The CAM-I Conceptual Design*, Boston, Mass, Harvard Business School Press: 1988.

Brody, Herb. "Overcoming Barriers To Automation," *High Technology*, May 1985, Vol. 5, #5, pp. 41-46.

Davis, Dwight B. "Apple: Harvesting The Macintosh," *High Technology*, May 1985, Vol. 5. #5, pp. 39-40.

———. "Renaissance On The Factory Floor," *High Technology*, May 1985, Vol. 5, #5, pp. 24-25.

DeYoung, H. Garrett. "GE: Dishing Out Efficiency," *High Technology*, May 1985, Vol. 5 #5, pp. 32-33.

Julian, Ken. "Westinghouse: Building A Better Board," *High Technology*, May 1985, Vol. 5, #5, pp. 36-38.

What's Happening in the United States?

Kinnucan, Paul. "IBM: Making The Chips Fly," *High Technology*, May 1985, Vol. 5, #5, pp. 34-35.

Marth, Del. "Keeping All Lines Open," *Nation's Business*, Oct. 1984, pp. 85-86.

Tucker, Jonathan B. "GM: Shifting To Automatic," *High Technology*, May 1985, Vol. 5, #5, pp. 26-29.

Page 163

13

The Hope for the Future

The goal of this book is:

To help the management of United States industry become more competitive in manufacturing facilities both in the United States and overseas.

To achieve this goal, this book has investigated other countries throughout the world in an attempt to:

1. Generate new ideas for U.S. managers by looking at other countries' management styles and production methods.
2. Help the U.S. manager understand his foreign competitors better.
3. Internationalize the U.S. manager by offering a multitude of alternative explanations and solutions to the same problem

These objectives were reached by studying many management systems from all parts of the world. Chapter 11 recaps these (CHART 11.1), and chapter 12 cites specific examples of how these techniques can be applied to industries in the United States. This latter chapter also highlights the strengths and weaknesses of the United States. Chapter 10 focuses on the ''fit'' of a management system to other cultures with varying goals. Chapters 2 through 10 point out that different countries have different goals and that the planning of a management system needs to incorporate and integrate all of these goals.

This book shouldn't leave you with the impression that a consultant once expressed—''Progress was good once but we've had just about enough of it.'' Quite the contrary. This book was written to recommend *new* directions for progress. Progress should be undertaken because it makes business sense to do so, and not just for the sake of automation or improved information. Those are *tools* toward solutions, not *reasons* for decisions.

Now, here are a few slogans to tack on your office walls:

- *It is better to eliminate than to automate.* The best improvement is simplification, not sophistication.
- *Labor-based cost systems are obsolete almost everywhere in the world.* Materials and machinery have become the critical scheduling elements.
- *The best way to beat competitors is to learn as much as possible about them.*
- *It's not so important where you stand as in what direction you're moving* (paraphrased from Oliver Wendell Holmes). We've been doing a little too much standing, as our productivity numbers indicate. It's time to get moving again.
- *All good ideas ultimately end up as a lot of hard work.* This is true of any of the management systems listed in this book. Implementation is rarely easy.

Unfortunately, there are those who feel that United States citizens don't hurt enough yet. When the hurt get's big enough, they'll get their act together and come back fighting. The last time this happened as a nation was in World War II. This is a sad testimony to American ingenuity.

An even sadder testimony is offered by those who say that the United States has gone from a nation of families to a nation of individuals. This implies that we have become too prideful and self-centered to work together, that we're only interested in "what's in it for me."

Enough negativism! American ambition can turn the productivity trends around. The turnaround needs to occur in management systems and attitudes as much as anywhere else. The tools listed in this book show us what techniques have been successful, and this book also provides information about where to go to learn more about the techniques you select. We must remember what a wise, old, highly-respected teacher once said:

Try!
There is no try.
Do or do not—
There is no try!

(Yoda, *The Empire Strikes Back*)

Index

Index

Other Bestsellers of Related Interest

COPYRIGHTS, PATENTS AND TRADEMARKS: Protect Your Rights Worldwide—Hoyt L. Barber

This practical how-to guide takes the complexity out of filing for copyrights, patents, and trademarks, helping you file your own applications without an attorney. It includes information and filing procedures for all 50 states, the District of Columbia, and more than 60 foreign countries! Hoyt Barber offers detailed explanations of ready-to-use copies of necessary forms and applications, and a complete listing of important addresses. You'll even learn how to design, register, and legally protect your own trademark. 272 pages. Book No. 30060, $15.95 paperback only

UNDERSTANDING WALL STREET— 2nd Edition—Jeffery B. Little and Lucien Rhodes

"An excellent introduction to stock market intracacies"—**American Library Association Booklist**

This bestselling guide to understanding and investing on Wall Street has been completely updated to reflect the most current developments in the stock market. The substantial growth of mutual funds, the emergence of index options, the sweeping new tax bill, and how to keep making money after the market reaches record highs and lows are a few of the things explained in this long awaited revision. 240 pages, 18 illustrations. Book No. 30020, $9.95 paperback, $19.95 hardcover

BUSINESSPERSON'S LEGAL ADVISOR—Cliff Roberson

Avoid legal problems and get the best legal advice when needed, at the least possible cost! This invaluable business guide covers: how and where to obtain licenses and permits; collecting accounts receivable, business insurance, product warranties, and disclaimers; hiring and dealing with attorneys; actions to take if your business is failing; and more. 240 pages, 19 illustrations. Book No. 2624, $14.95 paperback only

HOW TO INCORPORATE YOUR BUSINESS IN ANY STATE—Hoyt L. Barber

Now you can form your own corporation in any state without bureacratic hassles or expensive legal fees. Everything you need—including filing forms and other legal forms for all 50 states—has been included in this hands-on guide. 144 pages, Illustrated. Book No. 30044, $9.95 paperback only

COACHING FOR IMPROVED WORK PERFORMANCE—Ferdinand F. Fournies

"...a sorely needed guide/help book for sales-marketing managers."—**The Sales Executive**

Over 70,000 copies sold in hardcover; now available for the first time in paperback! By one of the nation's best-known business training consultants and specialist in coaching procedures, this book shows you face-to-face coaching procedures that allow you to obtain immediate, positive results with your subordinates. Filled with examples, case studies, and practical problem-solving techniques. Book No. 30054, $12.95 paperback only

FIGHT THE IRS AND WIN! A Self-Defense Guide for Taxpayers—Cliff Roberson

With this practical guide you can obtain the best results possible—protect your individual and property rights—in any dispute with the IRS. The outstanding feature of this book is that it takes complicated IRS operations and provides the average taxpayer with advice on how to protect himself in IRS controversies. It is the taxpayer's self-defense book. 224 pages. Book No. 30021, $12.95 paperback, $24.95 hardcover

CREDIT AND COLLECTIONS FOR YOUR SMALL BUSINESS—Cecil J. Bond

Here's a practical guide for busy entrepreneurs and credit managers that tells how to set up or overhaul a small credit department. Includes forms, applications, letters and reports ready to be copied and put to use. 192 pages, 66 illustrations. Book No. 30035, $18.95 paperback, $28.95 hardcover

SWISS BANK ACCOUNTS: A Personal guide to Ownership, Benefits, and Use—Michael Arthur Jones

There's a real misconception about Swiss bank accounts: everyone thinks they're only for rich people and criminals. This book is a complete guide to the *uses and benefits* of Swiss bank accounts, by a respected professor of finance and authority on the subject. It's a practical manual that shows readers how to choose, open, use, and maintain an account. All procedures are highlighted with sample forms, documents, and even sample correspondence. 230 pages. Book No. 30046, $21.95 hardcover only

AVOIDING PROBATE: Tamper-Proof Estate Planning—Cliff Roberson

Discover how to hand down everything you own to anyone you choose without interference from courts, creditors, relatives, or the IRS. In this easy-to-read planning guide, attorney Cliff Roberson shows how you can avoid the horrors of probate court. Sample wills and trust agreements and checklists in every chapter make planning each step easy. *Avoiding Probate* covers: living trusts, life insurance, specific property, wills, family businesses, valuing your estate, estate taxes, and more. 236 pages. Book No. 30074, $14.95 paperback, $29.95 hardcover

MONEY MINDER: Simplify, Organize, and Manage Your Personal Financial Records—Michael E. Feder

"I like (the book's) flexibility. The forms encourage you to think creatively and profitably about how you are spending and investing your money."—Jean Ross Peterson Author of Organize Your Personal Finances

Offers an excellent, streamlined method for straightening out your finances. This book offers step-by-step guidance and ready-to-use forms that will enable you to consolidate important financial facts and figures in one place. 128 pages, 88 illustrations. Book No. 30039, $12.95 paperback only

LENDING OPPORTUNITIES IN REAL ESTATE, A High-Profit Strategy for Every Investor—James C. Allen

Earn high yields at low risk by making short-term secured loans! This book offers specific advice and procedures for investing in short-term loans secured by real estate. Samples of actual forms involved are included. Topics addressed cover: preparing a personal financial statement, sources of free advice, borrowing investment capital, setting rates and terms in any market, advantages of smaller notes, avoiding foreclosure, and "prospecting" made easy. 192 pages, 42 illustrations. Book No. 30019, $24.95 hardcover only

EXPORTING—FROM START TO FINANCE—L. Fargo Wells and Karin B. Dulat

"In my thirty-five years of export experience this is the first book that was really helpful and answers some difficult questions.— **Ralph H. Chew,** National Federation of Export Associations and Chew International Group

Highly acclaimed by experts in international trade, this new book offers you everything you need to know to start a new export operation or improve an existing one. 460 pages. Book No. 30040, $39.95 hardcover only

INSTANT LEGAL FORMS: Ready-to-Use Documents for Almost Any Occasion—Ralph E. Troisi

By following the clear instructions provided in this book, you can write your own will, lend or borrow money or personal property, buy or sell a car, rent out a house or appartment, check your credit, hire contractors, and grant power of attorney—all without the expense or complication of a lawyer. Author-attorney Ralph E. Troisi supplies ready-to-use forms and step-by-step guidance in filling them out and modifying them to meet your specific needs. 224 pages, Illustrated. Book No. 30028, $15.95 paperback only

**HOW TO WRITE YOUR OWN WILL—
2nd Edition**—John C. Howell
"...a clearly written, helpful book."—**The
Newspaper,** Brookline, Mass.

A surprising number of people do not
prepare a will, mistakenly believing this vital
document is too expensive or too complicated to deal with. This book explains how
anyone can prepare a legal will without a
lawyer, without intimidation, at little
expense. All legal terms are defined and
sample forms are included. 208 pages. Book
No. 30037, $12.95 paperback only

**THE ENTREPRENEUR'S GUIDE TO
STARTING A SUCCESSFUL
BUSINESS**—James W. Halloran

Here's a realistic approach to what it
takes to start a small business. You'll learn
step-by-step every phase of business start-up
from initial idea to realizing a profit.
Included is advice on: designing a store lay-
out, pricing formulas and strategies, adver-
tising and promotion, small business
organization charts, an analysis of future
small business opportunities. 256 pages, 97
illustrations. Book No. 30049, $15.95
paperback only

Look for These and Other TAB books at Your Local Bookstore

To order call toll free 1-800-822-8158
(in PA and AK call 717-794-2191)
or mail coupon to TAB BOOKS Inc., Blue Ridge Summit, PA 17294-0840.

Title	Product No.	Quantity	Price

*Orders outside U.S. must pay with international
money order in U.S. dollars.*

☐ Check or money order enclosed made
  payable to TAB BOOKS Inc.

Charge my ☐ VISA ☐ MasterCard ☐ American Express

Acct. No. _____ Exp. _____

Signature: _____

Name: _____

Address: _____

City: _____

State: _____ Zip: _____

Subtotal $ _____
Postage and Handling
($3 in U.S., $5 outside U.S) $ _____
In PA, NY, & ME add
applicable sales tax $ _____

TOTAL $ _____

TAB catalog free with purchase; otherwise send
$1.00 in check or money order payable to TAB
BOOKS Inc. and receive $1.00 credit on your next
purchase.

**TAB Guarantee: If for any reason you are not
satisfied with the book(s) you order, simply
return it (them) within 15 days and receive a
full refund.**
BC